The Chasing Glance

The Chasing Glance

The Expression Garden

M S Yousafzai

authorHOUSE®

AuthorHouse™ UK Ltd.
1663 Liberty Drive
Bloomington, IN 47403 USA
www.authorhouse.co.uk
Phone: 0800.197.4150

Published by AuthorHouse   12/06/2013

ISBN: 978-1-4918-8606-9 (sc)
ISBN: 978-1-4918-8605-2 (hc)
ISBN: 978-1-4918-8607-6 (e)

Contents

Garden One

Garden Two

Garden Three

Garden Four

Garden One

MOTHER EARTH.

Don't be shy; you are so great to be high.
    You have given birth to us, we don't lie.

Your honour is raising everyday up to the sky.
    You grow every thing to feed children living by.

Sky covers you with spiritual power to supply.
    Rain of mercy comes down, so you not to die.

The Angels look at you, with their blessing eye.
    Scarp of clouds cover you, Mum don't be shy.

Mountains on your lap, they are tall standing high.
    Your pious children please you, other give you sighs.

O, Lord; bless the mother; accept our repent with genuine try.
    And except some Jinn and Men, all the birds, animals glorify.

We mankind and Jinn ask forgiveness for past annoy.
    Mother earth, you receive excellences from the sky.

You see cruel actions of Men, Jinn and tremble with tears supply.
    By our virtuous actions we are humble with fear from Lord High.

SKY, BLUE GARMENTS.

Sky wearing lovely blue garments, you standing tall.
 Looking for you, can't reach you, we are very small.

You are the Angels home and office, they never fall.
 Comparing to the earth, no body is paying tax and toll.

You are carrying all the beauty, stars, moon, sun and all.
 You have taken up Jesus all alive from the devil's call.

You spiritual treasure, souls first and after return to your hall.
 You are hosting all ancestors' souls in your great divine scroll.

You are wider; you are higher without any wall.
 You been very prouder in the glory, call my roll.

You are carrying; thunders, clouds and rain fall.
 You can shower burning fire, stones in few install.

All glorious Angel's known to you tall and small.
 They are proud in their own crowd young and all.

MOUNTAINS.

Gigantic body, you are standing all the time.
     Yours gushing rivers sprung from your spine.

You are carrying forest, rocks, and mineral mines.
     Yours body, beauty on the earth gives splendid shine.

You are bringing springs and falls well combine.
     You are hosting, monkey, birds, tigers and loin.

You are simple, real natural, a favourite of mine.
     You attract men and Jinn their lives spent are fine.

Some are rocky; some are smooth clay on line.
     Cool with snowfall, the rest hot with sun shine.

Yours proud inhabitant, a nice place to have dine.
     You are brown, dark and green with thinking sign.

You have seen all the history with decline.
     You have seen so many souls truly sublime.

Love your innocent paths, rocks, olives and trees of pine.
     Wow, your plants, trees, breeze and roaring voice line.

Sea Laugh.

Deep thoughts in the sea, I was walking on the sand.
     Huge waves on the move, I was thinking on the land.

I was really pondering in a wandering, what a force does attend?
     Sea size on the globe, think how many kinds inside of its bands.

Then stopped walking, turned to the sea on the sand.
     Answer from the sea, that I host much more than land.

Big waves roared with reply, I deep, wide than you understand.
     Much more creation of the Lord, I do board to keep my stand.

Sea then laughed at the land, why they fight to extend?
     Land was shy to reply, I regret for my own fighting hand.

I said you proud water, I agree whatever you explained.
     I shall pass on your words to keep some peace on the land.

I said yours bigger fish swallow the smaller, up to their stand.
     Sea replied I do not hide; they face the same for their errand.

Scary Graveyards

Change in the time brings difference like summer and winter.
    Range of the life is limited; everyday is like a life hunter.

The other day I walked by the graveyard just on its centre.
    Change in the time brings difference like summer and winter.

What has happened to them! Their souls are now with God's counter.
    Yes, range of the life is limited; everyday is like a life hunter.

I had worried feelings, about the last dealing of the Master.
    Change in the time brings difference like summer and winter.

Deformed graves and few decorated, as they were once monster.
    Range of the life is limited; everyday is like a life hunter.

I realized at that time once they were alive, God was their Pinter.
    Really, Change in the time brings difference like summer and winter.

Every one sees them, story of the past, now earth is their linter.
    Yes, range of the life is limited; everyday is like a life hunter.

No one can help them, their belief and actions are now their shelter.
    Really, Change in the time brings difference like summer and winter.

Paradise but a question for Hellfire also rises, ahead is a filter.
    Yes, range of the life is limited; every day is like a life hunter.

Candle's Tears

Light the flame of love, to keep it melt to the end.
　　You see what a candle does; sheds tears to defend.

We see light in result, when it is melting to the end.
　　Candle when you lit the flame, the dark is suspended.

You brightness of mine, excellent to see you sound.
　　Apart from all complaints, you the best I ever found.

I have seen candle burns it self to give light around.
　　I am sorry if I have blamed you without real ground.

To know the truth of mine you will say sorry in thousand.
　　Separation caused pains and cut on my heart has profound.

You tell the truth, who has all pains in life did extend?
　　Light the flame of our love, to keep it melt to the end.

Shy are you, loyal are you, why any more to pretend.
　　You see what a candle does; shed tears to defend.

Light the flame of love, to keep it melt to the end.
　　You see what a candle does shed tears to defend.

8

Don not, spy on me.

Oh, you blue eyes do not spy on me.
    Please, any tricks do not try on me.

Come along to heal, no more shy to me.
    Oh, you green eyes do not spy on me.

Come, you belong in the sky to me.
    Please, any tricks, do not try one me.

Yours sighs up in the sky reaches to me.
    Oh, you black eyes do not spy on me.

No more sadness, say hello hi, to me.
    Please, any tricks do not try on me.

You so true do not say good-bye to me.
    Oh, you brown eyes do not spy on me.

Let us prove the reality of you and me.
    Please, any ticks do not try on me.

Oh, you blue eyes, do not spy on me.
    Please, any tricks do not try on me.

That Bible.

I was shocked by looking at that Bible in the mud.
    I picked from the street, which affected my blood.

First I saw the street title Holly Bible in that flood.
    I was shocked by looking at that Bible in the mud.

People are gone so mean, that annoyed my head.
    I picked from the street, which affected my blood.

I picked up with respect, it was swallowed like bread.
    I was shocked by looking at that Bible in the mud.

Empty streets, I sensed from the sky some thread.
    I picked from the street, which affected my blood.

Really, stressed that night, had been thinking in bed.
    I was shocked by looking at that Bible in the mud.

Such a pity for the world, so much hearts are dead.
    I picked from the street, which affected my blood.

A shame for that devil who abused the Bible sacred.
    I was shocked by looking at that Bible in the mud.

<u>Broken Partner.</u>

Why marriages with love turn in remorse.
> What can be hurtful in life than a divorce?

Better to find out this remorse root source.
> Why marriages with love turns in remorse.

You need spiritual power against evil force.
> What can be hurtful in life than a divorce?

Intentions need to mention for love endorse.
> Why marriages with love turns in remorse.

Mind the past which is your learning course.
> What can be hurtful in life than a divorce?

Love wants attention in routine of course.
> Why marriages with love turns in remorse.

How hostility replaces promises of amorous.
> What can be hurtful in life than a divorce?

German Jinns

Old Germans were good in their practical Christianity.
    Our ancestors had seen their ancestor's nice hospitality.

We do not know; what made us so much nude celebrity.
    Old Germans were good in their practical Christianity.

Since we had teachings to participate in helping charity.
    Our ancestors had seen their ancestor's nice hospitality.

We totally now lost; we want back our old time serenity.
    Old Germans were good in their practical Christianity.

O, God guide us in religion, we have utterly lost reality.
    Our ancestors had seen their ancestor's nice hospitality.

Our ancestors had been living with morals and honesty.
    Old Germans were good in their practical Christianity.

We a nation of courage; our lives used to be in tranquillity.
    Our ancestors had seen their ancestor's nice hospitality.

We will lead the world in truth, we have that ability.
    Old Germans were good in their practical Christianity.

We do believe Allah will give us His help with facility.
Our ancestors had seen theirs ancestor's nice hospitality.

We were lost from the guidance, shame for obscenity.
Old Germans were good in their practical Christianity.

Let us cut the seed, good bye to all kinds of devil fertility.
Our ancestors had seen theirs ancestor's nice hospitality.

O Lord, forgive us, this world is a place of but mortality.
Old Germans were good in their practical Christianity.

The devils made some plans to plant within us hostility.
Our ancestors had seen their ancestor's nice hospitality.

Our ancestors had been departed, we had search for locality.
Their place was Afghanistan, we will answer others brutality.

Allah, we honestly accept Islam, make this ours speciality.
Old Germans were good in their practical Christianity.

We beg Allah, to keep us in Your path with normality.
Our ancestors had seen their ancestor's nice hospitality.

Chasing Glances

My glance everywhere chases you but finds illusion.
    Streets are full of people without you it is confusion.

The message of love once again to you is a revision.
    That waste is enough, can't afford more seclusion.

Treat our love with care, to carry on with a firm relation.
    Don't you see several years' efforts with out conclusion?

Produce the base and need for love with own contribution.
    I respect your feelings in your way then why this collision.

Let us grow more this love, an end to accusation.
    Bring love illustration to real, to see its illumination.

Cancellation to all whispers, to put by contribution.
    Give a good impression, to prove wrong speculation.

Imputation among us; causes in love a huge irritation.
    Why you see cooperation a source of degradation.

Re-imagination of annoy in past, cause attribution.
    Come to see in heart beat your love's compensation.

My glance everywhere chases you but finds illusion.
    Streets are full of people without you it is confusion.

Garden Two

<u>Religions!</u>

Be you and your religion that is I do not care.
      You and your dress, not bother what you wear.

Find the truth, if you got some time spare.
      I am not a preacher to make you scared.

What ever I believe, I never leave; I do bear.
      Divine instructions with restrictions, be aware.

Others respect with no suspect, I do share.
      God is Lord; others are fraud, if you hear.

In love of God; have you shed some tear?
      To one God, how other do you compare?

Entire human and Jen can't face one Angel, I swear.
      Why this growing rebellious society in world's rare.

Wealth, power and strength a dilemma of every dear.
      Why they mock divine Scriptures instead of own repair.

Politics and use of terms.

At least, I have not seen wisdom in this day ruling politician.
    Everywhere blood shed, oppression, they try new expedition.

The term, "Best interest of the nation", is their legal solution.
    At least, I have not seen wisdom in this day ruling politician.

Stressing news every day, killings, harassment is their notion.
    Everywhere blood shed, oppression, they try new expedition.

Communisms, fundamentalism and their terrorist hallucination.
    At least, I have not seen any wisdom in this day ruling politician.

These Paedophiles and crocodiles have been abusing God creation.
    Everywhere blood shed, oppression, they try for new expedition.

They play with civilians, as media is their ancestors' old station.
    At least, I have not seen any wisdom in this day ruling politician.

What is the reality of so-called democracy, intricacy is its foundation.
    Everywhere blood shed, oppression, they almost try new
    expedition.

They go round and round to save their seat for next election.
    At least, I have not seen wisdom in this day ruling politician.

The other half called opposition is null, with less succession.
    Everywhere blood shed, oppression, they try new expedition.

Politicians always need technicians to approve agenda permission.
    At least, I have not seen any wisdom in this day ruling politician.

Protests are useless as democracy is the source of obsession.
    Everywhere blood shed, oppression, they try new expedition.

By the name of best interest, innocent lives, wealth is omission.
    At least, I have not seen any wisdom in this day ruling politician.

POLLUTION.

Industrial revolution has given us wide pollution.
    Equally, inside it is breaking our moral notion.

No denial, many facilities have a good implication.
    But it has taken peace of mind and social relation.

Children and other access to porn, parents botheration.
    Atomic waste, auto smoke other needs reconsideration.

The entire world morally polluted, can be seen in every nation.
    Our life consists of body and soul but soul is facing isolation.

Noise and air pollution filled with false terror propagation.
    We are living all alone; that is a price for industrialization.

All religions are fighting and claim they got true divine revelation.
    All desire, then turn to God, to give an end to all religious pollution.

Every day run and run, nobody body has won, a bore competition.
    Rich and poor with growing ambition; living with tense relation.

More technology, destructive ideology a strengthening fashion.
    So called civilization; their hands are red with blood shed creation.

Wise.

Information is better than you give a surprise.
   To be sober and humble is better than a noise.

To be calm with patience is better and wise.
   Information is better than you give a surprise.

To be honest and true is as brighter as sun rise.
   To be sober and humble is better than a noise.

Observing silence is better than giving false promise.
   Information is better than you give a sudden surprise.

The blessings of the Lord and look at the Universe size.
   I say to be sober and humble is much better than a noise.

To be obedient servant is better than for making cries.
   Information is better than you give a sudden surprise.

Get satisfaction to keep up yours relatives ties.
   To be sober and humble is better than a noise.

Towards poor, needy and innocents do sympathise.
   Information is better than you give a sudden surprise.

To get spiritual touch, keep up practical pious tries.
   Really, to be sober and humble is better than a noise.

   If you true to the Lord, then keep equal if girls or boys.
   Information is better than you give a sudden surprise.

The Nationalist.

Every single person is a nationalist in his/her own way.
> The way of expression is different, what you shall say.

No harm to be a nationalist, rule needs to be obeyed.
> To be an honest specialist, serve your nation to pay.

Never neglect your own language, remember what I say.
> Education in your own language, avoid such a bad delay.

Tolerance, respect and faith in you, that is what I do pray.
> It is your own recognition as we are from the same clay.

Be realistic in your future decision, reject any evil play.
> Be optimistic in your life; in this world have a nice stay.

Both in religion and politics have a cup from divine bay.
> The world is just beneath your feet, have a glorious day.

Take an action with good intention; every day is your day.
> Be a humble servant of your Lord, pick from a heavens tray.

Children of today.

The first school is your house for education.
Family's behaviour is a source of foundation.

Teach your children morals, patience and devotion.
Have tolerance, with true belief to enjoy inhabitation.

The elders must respect their children in all situations.
Encourage to express them selves without degradation.

Use slight force if they use violent concentration.
Keep an eye to grow up some best social creation.

Within your control, to satisfy their expectation.
House is half of the part then school education.

Expensive materials are not a solution for destination.
Teach social contacts to strengthen relative's emotion.

Spiritual need is the same like physical condition.
Bear in mind to prepare for hereafter is no omission.

Once today's elders were children with imagination.
To day's children will be like elders grave station.

City after city.

In big cities vulgarity, barbarity around life is melting in the dark.
　　Parliaments, employments and solidarity are going for the
　　sharks.

Here everybody busy, unaware of neighbours like jungle park.
　　Traffic, rush yet much facilities attracts within its own mark.

People come to the cities for imaginary life to embark.
　　Now population is intense, even hard to find a car park.

City is a gushing place for the strangers, many here hark.
　　Yet in cities education, sports are bringing a good spark.

The serene lives of villagers see it uncontrolled noisy nark.
　　Apart from tourists, the residents thus give harsh remarks.

Look people are packed like chickens in houses, often they bark.
　　Noisy, drunken parentless neighbours, to the others never hark.

This pollution and illusion just for employment people here park.
　　I see pale and weary faces after work, what is then your remark.

Technicians plus Politicians.

Majority of this era politicians are most like predator crocodile.
　　　Conspirators in the state Agencies are like predator paedophile.

Hypocrisy is the centre of their rules, blood shed is their style.
　　　Such a hue about weapon of mass-destruction is their profile.

Lies upon lies; their propagated term terrorist is their mile.
　　　The whole world has seen the results; is their any denial?

Innocent nations are worried with the presence of these crocodile.
　　　Because of these paedophile and crocodile, now hard is survival.

Innocent nations are still red in blood, no body provided fair trail.
　　　These tow are worst than animals, some thing to burst
　　　meanwhile.

Before Jesus, there was Christianity in Europe, now it appears spoil.
　　　Even civilian blood has gone as cold, as their European blood
　　　royal.

Same colonist agenda, propaganda, weapons production is their style.
　　　Majority of this era politicians are most likely predators'
　　　crocodile.

They are sucking human blood but in public they wear smile.
　　　To support each other in their evil, they often give secret dial.

Interesting Jin.

Are you spying? And standing in the street like light post.
      Invisible creation, are you good Jin or one of the ghost?

Some are good, few are bad, or you guest or one of the host?
      Are you spying? And standing in the street like light post.

Are you living here or you came from North Sea coast.
      Invisible creation, are you good Jin or one of the ghost?

Some in Christmas like turkey but good is English roast.
      Are you spying? And standing in the street like light post.

She also said Scottish gas has burnt my neck and throat.
      Invisible creation, are you good Jin or one of the ghost?

French replied, they are back to graze their sheep and goat.
      Are you spying? And standing in the street like light post.

Regrets why we supported technicians politicians most?
      Invisible creation, are you good Jin or one of the ghost?

Christian children said we love music and Sunday toast.
      Are you spying? And standing in the street like light post.

No win for the sin, tomorrow is the day of believer boast.
      Invisible creation, are you good Jin or one of the ghost?

We are scared, changes on the horizon, about sinking boat.
      Are you spying? And standing in the street like light post.

We German miss green land, motorway, Mercedes almost.
      Invisible creation, are you good Jin or one of the ghost?

Some one Like Penguin.

Once dreaming life but now it has been ruined by some one.
Not only words but I want my share of the life as a lump sum.

Don't you hear my heart, you are my husband so-so handsome.
Once my dreaming life; now life has been ruined by some one.

I knew in last years, you walked in my streets like a penguin.
Not only words but I want my share of the life as a lump sum.

Then straight away come to my home, if you are a genuine.
Once dreaming life; now life has been ruined by some one.

Marriage meant to be excitement but I paid seven years ransom.
Not only words but I want my share of the life as a lump sum.

Years of hopes and yearns but I am gone pale in this boredom.
Once dreaming life; now life has been ruined by some one.

In the window of my heart, I have been watching some one.
Not only words but I want my share of the life as a lump sum.

His salutation in my garden but I made a fast and hard run.
Once dreaming life; now life has been ruined by some one.

I hide love from my love, he charged me for years ransom.
Don't you know you are only my loving husband handsome?

<u>In a slumber.</u>

In a way we were quarrelling, I still remember.
      I heard your innocent complaints in a slumber.

The days of loneliness are left to few numbers.
      I heard your innocent complains in a slumber.

Without you like fish in muddy river Humber.
      In a way we were quarrelling, I still remember.

I have not forgotten birth cards in December.
      I heard your innocent complains in a slumber.

What you think, you are in heart of my chamber?
      In a way we were quarrelling, I still remember.

Loss of love is waste of life like wasted bomber.
      I heard your innocent complains in a slumber.

Heart without pain is love in vain, cold chamber.
      In a way we were quarrelling, I still remember.

Officially known to you the month of November.
      Yes, I heard your innocent complains in a slumber.

Chanting Sparrow.

Yes, I melted my youth for several years in that sorrow.
   I was looking at the horizon for the hope of tomorrow.

Love is not a thing which any one can barrow.
   The other day I say a lonely chanting sparrow.

I never understood that moaning was so thorough.
   In deep thoughts I saw her heart was so hallow.

She said try to understand love not to swallow.
   She said hard to crush ambition and love to fallow.

I asked what is your story, what will you get tomorrow?
   I said o chanting come to me, not to die in water shallow.

What is Love?

Love, in my opinion the entire Ocean.
    Its water is a part for God with action.

Then divide the rest for other relations.
    Give its colors for wife but never mention.

Anchovies, Sardines and Turtle for parents with attention.
    Squid and Oysters are for decent flirt; with some restrictions.

Whales for worldly ambitions and lust if you trust in life fiction.
    Sea bass and trout are for brothers, sisters with true intention.

Shrimps and Lobster for uncles, unties with some donation.
    Then shark for charity, without show up and world's temptation.

Ocean waves for Angels, even Michael without heart infection.
    Cat fish and Monk fish for all humans with some attraction.

Sea horse and Dolphin and snakes for Jens with some contribution.
    For the rest of animals, sea plants with bulk and unique
    inspiration.

Of course its pearls and flowers for all good obedient children.
    Blue colors of Ocean for deceased ancestors as best compassion.

All beauty in the sea for all skies with its all attraction.
    Sea salt for the Angels holy horses in all skies sections.

Last but not least all taste birds and joy for young Angel's inspection.
    Its foam and winds are for all good reasons with some
    destruction.

The Grasp of Mighty Lord.

The Grasp of Lord is hard, so do not play with fire!
 The mercy of Lord is high but you never do inspire!

These so called civilized, promoters of insanity are born liars.
 This life is a test, once dead who can get another chance to hire.

This world, heavens and the whole universe is only God's Empire.
 Your belief and actions remain, while body die as soul never
 retire.

What ever knowledge and science we use, God is the only supplier.
 Once chance come to an end, then hopes of life do complete
 expire.

What has happened to instincts that your efforts never good acquire?
 Life is dear to all that is why the status of martyr is much higher.

Who brings clouds, rain, food, oxygen, is the universe employer.
 Can you see Angels, Jen, souls! Yet God is the owner of entire,

Earth quake, Tornado and storms, think as they happen, is not a satire.
 Beneath the earth some ruins, now your turn as in way of old
 choir.

EMPTY.

Empty streets, empty hearts and empty lives.
    Can you feel orphans cry and sadden wives?

Death is fact no escape, such a compromise.
    Don't you see funerals, tears and many cries.

Friends say a loved one while taking sighs.
    Memory dwells in heart which never dies.

Many say, Lord is mercy, while looking at the skies.
    Other says the deceased has gone just left behind ties.

Priest says in church, death is fact, even I will die.
    Further mentions verses, that paradise hosting joys.

Further priest warns about Hellfire to keep moral high.
    You mortal bodies, you will touch the grave as you die.

Oh Mighty Lord, forgive our sins, accept all these cries.
    Lord, we are none without Thy mercy, in van our tries.

A Decent Living Needs.

Money counts in life, do not allow extravagancy.
> Earn and spend in a way to fill sudden emergency.

Those betting, gambling and drugs are bad deficiency.
> As for charity you need moderation and pleasantry.

However, legal earning in a Godly manner is brilliancy.
> Without money even love life is struck by un-pleasantry.

The need of money can not be ignored for living occupancy.
> Do not be greedy, contribute tax and toll for your residency.

Evil earnings never bring peace of mind and Excellency.
> However, money can not buy everything by state agency.

If you give in the way of God, don't violate pocket efficiency.
> Do not deprive your own family in the race of divine captaincy.

To God, the volume and bulk is not measured in your currency.
> Intention, action is the measure of each soul growing Excellency.

Reality.

Truth is a reality; find out, some dreams are not like other dream.
    After a bright day, dark night is a reality for tomorrow life beam.

Those suppressed questions in your heart are a reality, a heating steam.
    Cattle eat green grass but provide white milk with yogurt, butter cream.

The past actions of the nations called history, is a reality with their name.
    God is the Judge; since many are dead that is a reality with a
    divine frame.

Treacherous words can not save; death is a reality with accepted shame.
    Tell either to laugh or weep for the fake religions of the people's
    claims.

Religious class point to others but the others to them with theirs blame.
    Once you spend your time, only actions will help, other excuses
    are lame.

Every day is a journey to death, you absorb some spiritual steam.
    Oh brothers and sisters keep away from evil, be in Godly steam.

Oh mankind do not think ill of Jens, they are the same from Creator stream.
    Let us pray for Jin and Men guidance, the Hellfire is the worst
    bathing dame.

God never forces religion; you are free in this world what ever faith to claim.
    Then after your life actions, Paradise and Hellfire is the result
    that reply came.

It is State responsibility to establish the divine scriptures commands as the same.
    Why then waste our life in a loss as we always prefer to throw on
    others blame.

State and The Concept of Freedom.

Solution for the world, how to get this state freedom concept?
  People with one language and same religion get easily accept.

Those with the same religion and language are living perfect.
  Many with the same religion but language different reject.

A mixture of languages does not suit; build your own state correct.
  Bring revolution for the truth, others agents in a way they react.

Then establish strong institutions, safe from politics intercept.
  Respect the law, as the institutes to remove any wrong suspect.

Welfare state for every nation, with strong justice aspect.
  Create influence free, departments in the state, with due respect.

Past elections, were bad fictions, get wise people to effect.
  In one religion do not allow facilitating other confusing sect.

No interference in other nations, unless nation gives a verdict.
  All land and wealth belong to God; don't be blood shed addict.

God is mighty, He created all entities with accountable sift.
  The glorious Angels write down your actions without theft.

Many like us came to this world, only actions they have left.
  Their accounts are with God, as to the other world death shifts.

Europe, one religion and one colour?

Why Europe has one religion and one colour on its ground?
>Seven thousand years ago their ancestors landed like crowned.

Father Noah, the ancestor, his life not less than hundreds years round.
>Abdul-Salaam left Germany with a number for Afghanistan to surround.

Father Noah sailed with his family, resulted Mediterranean drowned.
>After that wrath his followers children never thought to turn around.

That is why Europeans followed the divine Scriptures in one sound.
>I know father David and his son Solman appeared in Europe behind.

Alas! After Jesus his fabricated trail news reached to its soil un declined.
>Then Europe faced grisly tussles which never shone like ancestor shine.

The present occupiers have abondaned their ancestors Scriptures and mind.
>Now Europeans show themselves secular with a policy of a hunting hound.

Still some hope for tomorrow by their ancestor's spiritual past compound.
>My worry, the entire Europe acting against, they are un-spiritually inclined.

Do not forget, Europeans ancestors were saved, while for the other rained.
>That day the mercy of God turned in a wrath to get the rebellions drained.

Scriptures, legislations and reforms but for the storms Angels are trained.
>In past beneath the ground some towns with their nations got just framed.

Holy Father Adam.

Blessed entity, the first human was descended to the earth.
    He was sixty feet tall, with the mercy of God since his birth.

His birth without parents, from this clay increases my mirth.
    Why we all have forgotten his life an example of best worth.

That prostration of respect by Angels shows his status by birth.
    Blame yourself for your sins; do not throw on others your guilt.

For some time he resided in heavens, that mention is worth.
    Salutations to Father Adam, I do think about his strong health.

Why we turned hostile, his life and status is our wealth.
    Do not support evil, enmity of nations needs to get melt.

Think for a while about his thousands years life belt.
    I really feel hardships in his life, as I think in a depth.

We are so ashamed by neglecting our Father Adam cult.
    Today you are some one because of him, have you felt?

He a Messenger, our father, my love before him knelt.
    He a miracle himself, salutations is to him from earth.

COMMON FARMERS.

You are struggling all the year growing crops for us.
　　And we are wasting fruit and veg, big loss for us.

You working so hard; watching every plant for us.
　　You never get proper price; you provide grant to us.

Regardless of weather, working so much long for us.
　　In hot and cold, you sowing fields all belong to us.

Watering field, cutting it; your efforts never less.
　　Apart from fruit and Veg you grow grain to bless.

Crops, Cattle, meat, leather and milk produce for us.
　　You face much hardship, o believer you are blessed.

Wow, you love the soil; she loves you never less.
　　If you don't spend time with her, she always misses.

You do love your soil, she feels a natural kiss.
　　I say o believer farmer; you both have bless.

Creation of Accountability?

Humans and Jen are accountable to God, with their choice free.
    Since, God has been given guidance, you can see from Adam tree.

Then we created disputes in religions, on which we did not agree.
    Both Jen and Men carry instinct, knowledge with heavenly decree.

So many Prophets, Scriptures but many of us watch like a referee.
    Faith, belief come first and your actions record folded history.

Free choice in this life, what to believe but death is a last entry.
    Every single action shall be presented on that day, we do agree.

Paradise or Hellfire is for both with their checkable summary.
    Next day of life is a step, towards another life in so such hurry.

We have seen people of power, good and bad with past discovery.
    A realized fact for every one, that dark graves alone are very scary.

Jen and Men can build a society with rules and law extra ordinary.
    Animals free from here after, as their potential is not of a degree.

Angels too are bound to the limits with a clear divine boundary.
    Angels, Men and Jen are high to the Lord, in their own obligatory.

Free choice to spend life but eternal life is then a resulting salary.
    History of the past in Scripture tells a real divine unfolding story.

Sins, cruelty, oppression then what to expect from exalted glory.
    Fear of God, true faith in your life then you wouldn't get so worry.

Skies.

It makes me wonder as I see the blue wide skies.
    The lovely color of heavens is pleasing my eyes.

The sun, moon, stars; shine all above very high.
    Thinking about the universe is cooling my eyes.

The whole universe has been covered by skies.
    My heart pumps with joy as more finds my eyes.

Divine commands, Angels, clouds come from the skies.
    Concentrate to explore the signs of Lord, you living by.

As we think of Allah, our eyes raise to the skies.
    The Angels also keep record of us in the skies.

When we are asleep, our souls go up in the skies.
    Soul experiences wondering, which pleases eyes?

Blue the color of love, spiritual so lovely skies.
    Those shining stars, moon is pleasing my eyes.

Allah sends commands from above the seventh sky.
    As I look above to the supreme power, can you deny?

Garden Three

Learn to Laugh?

Love; no more tears, give it stop.
    I am yours, come learn to laugh.

When love in hands, you never drop.
    Love; no more tears, give it stop.

Your value on my heart beats top.
    I am yours, come learn to laugh.

Beauty increases when you wear scarf.
    Love; no more tears, give it stop.

Harmonize your nature even half.
    I am yours, come learn to laugh.

Explain complaints to clean with mop.
    Love; no more tears, give it stop.

Bye sorrows, now harvest your crop.
    I am yours, come learn to laugh.

Attention, the edge of words is sharp.
    Love; no more tears, give it stop.

Why to Ignore?

When love stands at the thresh hold of your door,
    Tell; do you really enjoy to shed tear and ignore.

When love is gone, don't you feel moments turn so bore?
    A mystery, to remember harsh words only in heart's store.

When you deprive yourself, then why search to explore,
    No healer can help, when love is not by you any more.

When you wait for years then you spoil love to the floor,
    You lose your health; lose your wealth like boat off shore.

In all efforts of love the warm cordial feelings to you I adore,
    Whatever responsibility is left on your side, need to be restored.

Be optimistic for tomorrow, here comes to you my assure,
    In spiritual world of my love, you are young as ever more.

Your soul mate, also presents on the heaven love singing roar,
    Let me to inform every body, only you have been my allure.

Pink, Yellow or Blue.

I can not stay like this any long?
    To say, you to me only belong.

I have seen true love is only strong.
    I can not stay like this any long?

Make correction if I am wrong?
    To say, you to me only belong.

So bore without you each throng.
    I can not stay like this any long?

It is for you, my love is not slang.
    To say, you to me only belong.

Don't you listen to my singing song?
    Love, I can not stay like this any long?

I fancy pink, yellow or blue dress with my clang.
    To say, you to me only belong, to me only belong.

Eastern Marriages in the West.

Many Eastern married in Europe to have their life chill.
　　After some time it was hard to pay expenses and bill.

Many said they are married like a stressful spell.
　　In East they were bosses at home, now need a skill.

Other said we miss our village, streets and water Mill.
　　Many obsessed by suspicions to plan a partner kill.

Western partners try to discipline their imported hell.
　　Many abstained from violence as police is another shell.

Contrast in mentality and cultural distance was another thrill.
　　Whoever I have asked, they replied by God, life is really nil.

In village it was mustard for hair but here it is sticking jell.
　　We are engaged to mortgage for the rest of life working drill.

Wives in the West are like knives, says those married hell.
　　Wives say they do mess around and drink what else to tell.

Complain Eastern husbands are harsh to understand wives will.
　　Western expects permission to your room with salutation swirl.

She needs a submissive husband otherwise he is a boring smell.
　　By the end many enforce a divorce you can see their eye swell.

Let be.

Let be, simplicity and truth your life fashion.
  Have generosity of mirth with love emotion.

Let be, the first priority faithful love ambition.
  Let be, simplicity and truth your life fashion.

Let be, life understanding with best impression.
  Have generosity of mirth with love emotion.

Let be, very close forever with true expression.
  Let be, simplicity and truth your life fashion.

Let be, prosperous within wife, husband relation.
  Have some generosity of mirth with love emotion.

Let be, one soul and body with out any treason.
  Let be, simplicity and truth our best life fashion.

Let be, a grown up parents with next life mission.
  Have some generosity of mirth with love emotion.

Not a Flirt?

You supposed to be my husband, not a flirt?
Male dominate society, do you feel my hurt?

Marriage holy bond, it is not a changing shirt!
You supposed to be my husband, not a flirt?

That waste of golden years, now to alert.
Male dominate society, do you feel my hurt?

We meant to be one body, why we on divert?
You supposed to be my husband, not a flirt?

Heart pains, loss of youth, we useless expert.
Male dominate society, do you feel my hurt?

Message for everybody, avoid life from avert.
You supposed to be my husband, not a flirt?

Thanks, my love has been with you in concert.
Male dominate society, do you feel my hurt?

Flame, not a spark.

I want a bright life, not that dark.
    Show me your flame not a spark.

I want a reality with its true mark.
    I look for a human one not a shark.

I want a love with morals, not a bark.
    Want a divine pasture not a dry park.

Complain but a pleasant one, not a stark.
    Want to drink a full bottle, not its cork.

I want to offer reconcile not a nark.
    Appreciate without abusive remark.

For blinds a sunny day is still a dark.
    Don't you see a light without spark?

Then join true caravan, not a lost embark.
    I want true simplicity, not a false remark.

What you Guess?

Guess a divine kiss, to carry on life without stress.
 You are the one, do forgive, tell me don't you miss.

Those buried words in your heart, speak to bless.
 Those wrong incidents in love, that was not harass.

Both were right, that was only our bashful dress.
 Then stay together, never bother, do love express.

You are fine; get him online but never less.
 Get heart combine, no more walk on reverse.

Sky is there, earth is there, why hopelessness.
 Sun is there, moon is there, why still loneliness.

No more shy, do you still deny! What is this?
 You and me, me and you, did you never guess.

Love on one side, but that innocent look does impress.
 Emotion needs words, does not help to keep suppress.

That Killing Loyalty.

Make me understand about that killing loyalty.
      That mad-some your stand about partner royalty.

Silent days in the past were strange hostility.
      That avenge-some approach was abnormality.

Hands on heart I acknowledge most of your quality.
      Would you ignore all this written calling quality?

Let us today I show some love hidden ability.
      Real love in this beating heart is your specialty.

You are like shadow with me, in this serenity.
      My life events remember you in each activity.

Do forgive me, for not providing any facility.
      Re-think of that winter about rare availability.

In some stage, you will see some of my tranquility.
      I wish to present you the rest of life with hospitality.

Mishandle Marriages.

The worst pains of one's life when your marriage is mishandle.
　　The life dark days and nights when extinguished is your candle.

Show compassion to your love, it concerns really very gentle.
　　The worst pains of one's life when your marriage is mishandle.

Smoking and drinking can not give you relief for sorrows bundle.
　　The life dark days and nights when extinguished is your candle.

Why trust disappears, tiny things reflect to you like big scandal.
　　The worst pains of one's life when your marriage is mishandle.

Tragedy, as love is shown to a lover, other behaves like a mental.
　　The life dark days and nights when extinguished is your candle.

Once heart is broken, who to get its pieces re-assembled?
　　The worst pains of one's life when your marriage is mishandle.

You will forget other loss but love loss is life time going muddle.
　　The life dark days and nights when extinguished is your candle.

Charm.

You by my side, you are life charm.
　　You are my destiny, it keeps me calm.

Those pleasant days of life keeps hope warm.
　　Such turbulence, still love remains un-harm.

Blames come in love like un-wanted storm.
　　No more shadows of sorrows, after reform.

Show courage to change life and lines of palm.
　　Don't conceal your love in heart let me inform.

Everybody needs improvement to achieve wanted form.
　　I agree that a love word to lover is like charity and alms.

My tribute in your way; patience has been your norm.
　　Then keep fighting for truth sorrows need to be des-armed.

So lovely your dress?

Those killing looks; how lovely your dress?
    That sparking smile, each kiss gives bless.

My prayer always with you, live without stress.
    Those killing looks; how lovely your dress?

Your secrete qualities are keeping impress.
    That sparking smile, each kiss gives bless.

Don't mistake my love as acts of harass?
    Those killing looks; how lovely your dress?

Love needs attention as tender watercress.
    That sparking smile, each kiss gives bless.

Lover wants love; not a language of suppress.
    Those killing looks; how lovely your dress?

Honey bee, here comes in your way my regrets.
    O God, that sparking smile, each kiss gives bless.

Honey Bee.

Oh soul's partner fly with me to the heavens sight.
    The world is dark but in heavens it is ever bright.

Don't be shy, that bashful dress of moral is nice gait.
    We all will get together then in heavens life is all right.

Come to explore together why we lost all divine light.
    Broken love, life in separation is not less than nail bite.

To recover from life pains, get back all life excites.
    Marriage is not a thing like changing affair spite.

Life needs courage with a change of black and white.
    Wake up from comma gain some spiritual guide light.

You are never ignored, this love been on your left right.
    Oh my extinguished candle let us for loves do re-alight.

Honeybee, my protest did love not a fail deceit.
    Expression of love in my garden is heart delights.

Fairy lady if he regrets then why you don't invite?
    Tears in love, then why you selected hurtful fight?

Just Abuse only.

Do realize girl and boy friend relationship is only an abuse?
    If some one truly in love, why not get marry without excuse.

Many spoil their lives in search and form character loose.
    They face hunt after hunt but never get honest propose.

Calm down, yet you are young to partner choose.
    The best known are relatives and other so close.

This so called freedom has saddened innocent to their nose.
    All divorces and sexually transmitted diseases do oppose.

Usually, these so called friends introduce to drug doze.
    Then pain after pain, they start thinking of hanging hose.

Humans are not to deal like a pair of throwing shoes.
    Tell do you have some courage to get rid of all abuse?

Why each person so attractive then tears after expose!
    Brother and sisters the choice is yours without impose.

Music.

Decent music for every body is not so bad!
 Do you know! Singing garden make me glade.

Other noisy, rubbish stuff is almost mad.
 Simple music is the best in each decade.

Vulgar, nonsense also annoy lover, Mum and Dad.
 In real garden Adam Khan to Abdurrahman has paid.

Rehman Baba used to play; Rabab to love invade.
 Comparing other poetry to R-Baba is bad lost trade.

Never thought about poetry, now read this shade.
 Khan's Gardens bring healing touch to lady and Lad.

Moderation for reformation, not usual blade.
 Grow your character and trade in each arcade.

My love and complements to loving Jens in all parade.
 Among Humans and Jens reward comes with its grade.

In dreams

Honey, you always has been a part of my dream.
     So amazing, I never heard from you any scream.

You are flowing in my thoughts like a stream.
     Do you feel now a day around my soul's steam?

There is another book of mine tells true dream like cream.
     That may be shocking for the world, no body has ever seen.

Are you blind! Yet eyes are not needed for divine beam.
     Nothing is sarcastic it is all about good universal mean.

Every day I see guilty crowd, could you also deem.
     On the other hand, lucky birds and animals are seen.

From the Lord I asked my love without growing flame.
     Really, under divine light I do feel some time shame.

My regards for all loving Jens as they are ever clean.
     They show their love in a number of my written dreams.

Among our young Jen brother and sister present their claim.
     Sequel, in the ranks of Angels they have received their name.

Scratch On My Heart.

The scratch from your hands on my heart I remember.
Oh! Your love becomes a nightmare in my slumber.

I missed you; I missed you in wasted year's number.
She said you did not return my head was in surrender.

You went away upset; each day went under a thunder.
She said it is not only you, I accept my stupid blunder.

He said Belinda was so blind in each love reminder.
God is witness I was kind with considering encounter.

He said I have not forgotten that room, box, letter and winter
Also that swallowed face, that silly gape from heart center.

She asked you never talked about love, now a chanter.
He said, love for you, neither I neither am hunt nor wild hunter.

59

Keep me in your feelings.

Please, don't keep me out of your feelings.
  Few words from your lips are my healings.

Yours smiling, gentle touch are my dealings.
  Please, don't keep me out of your feelings

Don't hide your pretty smile in that veiling.
  Few words from your lips are my healings.

Fill this empty heart with your lovely speaking.
  Please, don't keep me out of your feelings.

So, thirsty my soul for yours company breezing.
  Yes, few words from your lips are my healings.

Would you acknowledge in past my greetings?
  Please, don't keep me out of your feelings.

Does, maturity in life teach some appealing?
  Then, few words from your lips are my healings.

You in my Lap.

Honey, do you really mean that escape.
    Don't you want your soul in my lap?

Don't you want to remove all that gape?
    Have you forgotten the street of my map!

Don't you realize our several years misshape?
    Tell how tears come down from heart's scrap.

Love is sincerity, not a source of a trap!
    Try and try again if seems like sour grape.

Is it illegal, if love gives one and a half slap?
    Come to me then see in my eyes your shape.

Then don't be shy to enjoy those hands clap!
    Each beat of my heart wants you in my lap.

Cage.

Do you remember when I wrote your name on my life page?
  Do you remember when you selected life like a bird in cage?

I remember my soul searches yet some time outrage.
  Do you realize those days and now this passing age.

Yesterday and today with loss; tomorrow must not be mirage.
  Look out yourself in my heart; nothing is late in this stage.

Keep me close to your heart like identity badge.
  What has surprised you, I supposed to be real sage.

To this homeless one, in your heart bestow some refuge.
  Tell me exactly, do you want the reality of my hearts wage.

Oh my partner, you the only one, the rest are just spoilage.
  Would you be happy to keep you lock in my heart's cage.

Scallop in an Ocean.

Don't get pathetic, have some pleasure for yourself.
    No hesitation, come across if you need some help.

Not only you, am I also responsible for that gulf.
    Eat the fruit without stone, just enjoy sweet pulp.

You are an answer to my imagination as a scalp.
    I don't know why you have been doll in a shelf.

Love is like Ocean; matrimonial is one of its scallops.
    Wisdom will answer how you will need to re-develop.

Be on right direction, yet practical steps with action gallop.
    Oh, beloved re-read my letters not merely its envelope.

Flowers and Thorns.

I cultivated flowers in my dream world; thorns came in my way.
  Whatever I have planned in my life nothing happened but delay.

Listen, I poured the cup of my heart in your way.
  Is it not enough! Or something else I should say.

Then I cultivated each love word in Garden bay.
  Then each blossom smiled at my love day by day.

Then I saw divine signs and waited for the grant of my pray.
  I looked at the heavens like thirsty land for some spray.

Oh, God why all delights is gone from me so astray.
  On times I raised my eyes to heavens with humble pray.

Why love life has turned like gamble or like sporting play.
  I have been really faithful why it was deemed like betray.

That time gape so sad; not good for any kind of survey.
  Always, it has been your choice either to lose or to stay.

What true love means to me that is left to God for best convey.
  Beauty of body and character belong to privacy not to display.

Yourself in my eye.

Why you don't see yourself in my eye?
    Don't you know, without you I will die?

Don't you listen to my hearts why and why!
    Don't you confess you are only my and my.

Don't you feel my each ambarcing try and try?
    You know on occasions I have been really shy.

Don't you listen our souls speak on the sky!
    Now compensate my sorrows and each cry.

Don't you be grateful other than to sigh!
    This world love is a shadow the other is high.

Don't you want a paradise and to fly!
    Find the doors to paradise then apply.

Pay attention to whatever is told and comply.
    No mathematics but on divine force to rely.

Be serious, it is neither joke nor any sort of lie.
    In reality Expression Garden is unreachable by.

True Heart.

True are you, true your love; I need to hear.
    My o my companion, you do not need to fear.

I know, I know, in love you shed some tear.
    True are you, true is your love, I need to hear.

With out flirt, yours true heart, come to share.
    My o my companion, you do not need to fear.

People are jealous, do not care; just feel me near.
    True are you, true is your love, I need to hear.

I blame you; you are staying away, oh my dear.
    My o my companion, you do not need to fear.

Smooth are you, smooth your love like river.
    True are you; true is your love I need to hear.

You are the chosen; eventually you are the winner.
    I do feel your feelings, break all worry and fear.

True are you, true is your love, I need to hear.
    My o my companion, you do not need to fear.

Carry me.

Carry me as close, as you use to carry school bag, oh my heart.
  Read me, like your books to know how to extinguish love thirst.

Hold me to heart as you used to hold your pen in the first.
  Carry me as you use to carry school bag, oh my heart.

Also, remember the days, you used to moan with a heavy heart.
  Read me like your books, to know how to extinguish love thirst.

Explore me, as you used to wonder in your heart.
  To live in a way, whatever pleases you in the best?

  Ha-ha, ha-ha, now you know our feelings, so lovely, so lovely.
  Be carefree from the rest of the world, the world is so ugly so ugly.

Now, with you towns and gardens seems so lovely so lovely.
  Be carefree from the rest of word, they so ugly, so ugly.

Oh, you honey divine, come to me without worry and hurry.
  You and me to remove all annoy and keep it burry and burry.

Shinning Glass.

I may pick all the thorns in life from your way.
      Oh, you shining glass of mine now let me say.

Heart is full of warmth that is what to convey.
      Oh, you shining glass of mine now let me say.

Posses my love with a condition not to betray.
      I may pick all the thorns in life from your way.

Prove, whatever you always claim to say.
      Oh, my darling, I am ready forever to pay.

We, asking divine guidance, not to go astray.
      To have flourishing, strengthen love I do pray.

I assure, what you want, you the one to sway.
      Bestow your feelings on me, like raining spray.

Approach to me with a tender feeling to convey.
      Avert all the storms of sorrow, with a blessing say.

I may pick all the thorns in life, from your way.
      Oh, you shining glance of mine, now let me say.

Dream Shadow.

Love, you walk in a dream like shadow with me.
You attune the beam of loving meadow with me.

By departing so early, you just kill, with out killing me.
Cease the estrange response, to expel that burning me.

You are my mirth and whim so essential to me.
Love, you walk in a dream like shadow with me.

Engrave a buzz, as to furnish a role, like honeybee.
You attune the beam of loving meadow with me.

You the depth of my heart, so exquisite to me.
Love, you walk in a dream like shadow with me.

If you like anytime, perturb when you want me.
You attune the beam of loving meadow with me.

In dream my soul searching you, is so dear to me.
Love, you walk in a dream like shadow with me.

In life, whatever, I fond you the one near to me.
You attune; the beam of loving meadow with me.

Love, you walk in a dream like shadow with me.
You attune the beam of loving meadow with me.

<u>Pardon me.</u>

To sprinkle petals of love, would you be pleased?
 If you say no to my love, heartbeat shall be ceased.

Day and night my feelings for you are enshrouded.
 Either you know or not, you have been so proud.

Still you do not hear my heart hue and cry so loud.
 I can't see you as I can't see the sky with cloud.

Going day-by-day, so sensitive, you still so annoyed?
 Pardon me, if you still with ambitious enigma terrified.

Enrich to resume, which in life has been rectified.
 Not to offend, annoy to suspend, worry falsified.

You dwell in my heart garden; I am still satisfied.
 You luster in my garden, are you still annoyed?

You shining star, as sky clear from the cloud.
 The love we have shared, I am still so proud.

Flower with Fragrance.

Only true love remains with its own mark.
　　　Better to know, how high raises its spark.

Don't steal, what you feel, that is a side dark.
　　　Need devotion, to flourish and avoid stark.

For natural love, you need a natural life to talk.
　　　No temptation but real companion in life to walk.

Relax to reconcile between, whatever you strike,
　　　Revoke the hurdle of path, whatever you strike.

Rely on your love and inner feeling of soul to link.
　　　What an answer comes from conscience you think.

Check the track, of true love in life to bask.
　　　Always true love remains with its own mark.

Pick a flower with a fragrance that is to ask.
　　　Better to know, how high is raising the spark.

Only true love remains with its own mark.
　　　Better to know, how high raises its spark.

Our Hearts Connections.

My love to see you gloomy it drowns me really.
   To find you cheerful, I feel that breeze personally.

Your smile gives compassion exceedingly.
   Our heart connection strengthens rapidly.

To have your consent in every step particularly.
   To find you cheerful, I feel that breeze personally.

You capture now my heart, to know it specially.
   My love to see you gloomy, it drowns me really.

I admire your suffering in love, like me precisely.
   To find you cheerful, I feel that breeze personally.

Come to ablaze all pains and annoy in love happily.
   My love to see you gloomy, it drowns me really.

Consider now to reassure our love in life normally.
   To find you cheerful, I feel that breeze personally.

Your rare silky looks, in my way to grow specially.
   To find you cheerful, I feel that breeze personally.

Your smile gives compassion exceedingly.
   Our hearts connection strengthens rapidly.

Khaperai-

Khaperai, this heart is fragile, come speak to me.
    Pretty your looks and smile, truly seek for me.

When you are annoyed, every thing so bleak to me.
    How intense are my feelings, come and look at me.

Khaperai, inspire to fly, you so love sick to me.
    With out a word, through your breath invoke to me.

Khaperai, if guilty, then in your heart lock up me.
    You are heavenly required, to inspire, look at me.

Khaperai, if you hide your heart, so weak to me.
    From sorrow to liberate, all customs break for me.

Khaperai, this delaying to contact, like hook to me.
    Why it is taking too long, for a word and look at me.

Khaperai, this heart is fragile, come speak to me.
    Khaperai, pretty your looks and smile, seek for me.

Compensation.

Your charm for my heart is like assassination.
    Your love and care instead is its compensation.

To be with you for life a distinguish imagination.
    Your charm for my heart is like true assassination.

True love, to prove needs our real combination.
    Your love and care instead is like compensation.

A walk in countryside brings more sensation.
    Your charm for my heart is like assassination.

True nature looks prettier with your inspiration.
    Your love, care, instead is like life compensation.

Holiday with a love tour brings more concentration.
    Your charm for my heart is like real assassination.

In a holiday, to express love with confidence grows combination.
    Take a time, away from noise, glamour to strengthen foundation.

Stubbornness in relation brings up more exasperation.
    Your love and care, instead is like my compensation.

Prevent all negligence to avoid cruel separation.
    Your charm for my heart is like real assassination.

Rebuke all mistrust and annoying self-concentration.
    Your love and care, instead is like my compensation.

CRUSH OR CARE.

I have laid-down my heart in your way, what you prefer.
Are you going to crush it, either you would take its care.

I expect you kind and mindful would take its care.
My heart trembles, as I do not have a chance to hear.

Some time your negligence is cruel, that is what I fear.
I have laid-down my heart in your way, what you prefer.

True love is not only physical, its origin is interior.
The moments I spent with you in love are superior.

Oh, my love as I see around, true love is so rare.
High moral and devotion; to nourish love with tear.

True love is vital, as it forms a generation in days near.
This love brings up a family of yours, you must take care.

Pure love, free from vulgarity is better, if you compare.
Everlasting joy for the whole life with its fruitful share.

Loving heart rhythm with attention forms nice atmosphere.
My love to be a life partner with norms is sweeter.

I have lay-down, my heart in your way, what you prefer.
Are you going to crush it either you will take its love care.

Train Station.

Ha, do you remember, that day at the train station?
    I am still thinking and surrounded by that emotion.

You turned away all my love world and imagination.
    Even you never tried to have a simple conversation.

You just crushed my love by changing path direction.
    Do not blame me, rethink about the continuing friction.

What a shame, when you abuse love with intention.
    All the pains given by you, some to be mentioned.

If I deal you in the same way what will be your situation.
    What a pity, you preceded for our marriage fluctuation.

Tell, what made you ignore always my invitation?
    To have a single contact been for you degradation.

Life been difficult without you, with lonely habitation.
    Yours baseless allegation has caused more irritation.

My love always stopped me from love assassination.
    Do you remember that day at your local train station?

Many times been at your doorsteps for reconciliation.
    You have always been haughty to realize our situation.

Your childish response shall be remembered by generation.
    Regret, tears cannot replace those pains and degradation.

The Broken Heart to Combine.

To day in my head, memories are coming like a rain.
    My love, unknowingly you have affected my brain.

Recalling, all those memories make me insane.
    Do not know you are affecting my heart frame.

I don't know really either to give you entire blame.
    Rather to distinguish you with a factious love name.

Being hurt fallen in my own homeland love town.
    Thirsty swallowed and still hungry in my love garden.

Today refreshing memories with love and pain.
    My love, unknowingly you have affected my brain.

O life partner, be strong to break all that strain.
    To day in my head, memories are coming like rain.

All towns seem deserted with out love of mine.
    As we get together, forever our life is then fine.

Without you, my life is empty, seems like shrine.
    My love you come, to get the broken heart combine.

Legal and Real Love.

Find legal and real love, which gives a good taste.
    If you think, selfish lust in life is almost your waste.

Be mindful to find satisfaction in legal loyal chaste.
    Be civilized, anything apart has to constantly distaste.

Haram, relations in life making things worst.
    Stealing others honor, some thing will burst.

Proud your children if parents have been living chaste.
    The other way round, then shame is sticking like paste.

Find the difference between animals and human taste.
    If same like animals that is what heavens has detest.

If you say, I do love, then why in this shameful state.
    From boy and girl friend drama every body is frustrate.

Did you hear important matter, some body has located.
    You are a part of society, play your role to advocate.

Find the reality of life and extinguish your thrust.
    Many will deny but one day the truth will burst.

Nothing is Late in Improvement.

Never get late in love to heal burns and pains.
>Your truth forever with love concern remains.

Go ahead, a positive turn in love maintains.
>Never late in love to heal burns and pains.

Delay in improvement causes in love curtains.
>Your truth forever with love concern remains.

Go ahead love in abundance like shower and rains.
>Think; be never late in love to heal burns and pains.

I have seen the effect of delay with stress and strain.
>Really, your truth forever with love concern remains.

Your concern has been every single day like a burden.
>With out you I found my heart weeping in love garden.

Still a step, it is never late to cure your lover pains.
>Of course, truth forever with love concern remains.

Enchanting.

In a blue sky like dewdrops on grass in the morning.
You in your blue dress seem to me as moon shining.

Both you and sky seems equally compelling.
But you are the flower with dewdrops smiling.

You are sweetie; your looks are so charming.
Charming yours looks, with a love everlasting.

Yours love compelling gestures are so pleasing.
When you are away, appetite for you is raising.

As you walk and look at me that is too enchanting.
You my love are anytime in life so ever wanting.

Cool is that atmosphere, where you are breathing.
Feelings are higher where you and me are reaching.

Dreams are so sweeter, as we have a glancing.
Moments are so dearer, as we have a glancing.

Everything so nearer, as we in love are sparkling.
The heartbeats are melodious, as you are wanting.

HUM, HUM.

If you want to know my love then, come, come.
　　My love until now, known to you just some, some.

Think, what bother you about me, to come, come.
　　My love until now, known to you just some, some.

I am lying down my heart for you, just come, come.
　　To bring support to you also bring your, mum, mum.

You just talking to yourself, let us have fun, fun.
　　If you want to know my love, then come; come.

My darling, call me, email me, with a hum, hum.
　　My love until now, known to you just some, some.

No more hesitation, you know my home to come, come.
　　Bring certification; you know the tune with hum, hum.

Love of the garden, color of the pardon, just come, come.
　　That is until now in love known to you, just some, some.

If you want to know my love, then come; come.
　　My love until now, known to you just some, some.

Do not leave me alone?

My love, next time do not leave me here alone.
　　Please, do not leave me in that bothering tune.

Why so angry, not calling me on my own phone.
　　It is worrying when I do not see you until noon.

Speak to me; meet with me, in our love zone.
　　My love next time, do not leave me here alone.

Do promise me that you will come back soon.
　　Please, do not leave me in that bothering tune.

Bright star on the sky, I find you in the full moon.
　　My love next time, do not leave me here alone.

When I kiss you that reminds me of holy stone.
　　Please, do not leave me in that bothering tune.

Why you seem so quiet, this freeze to be thrown.
　　My love, next time does not leave me here alone.

My moonlight I do enjoy what you have shown.
　　Please, do not leave me in that bothering tune.

<u>Regrets.</u>

Thanks; you kept my love in heart secrets.
  I wrongly suspected, do accept my regrets.

Thanks for your love, to feel our life threats.
  I wrongly suspected, do accept my regrets.

You have been looking to find me in streets.
  Thanks; you kept my love in heart secrets.

You been day and night in my heart beats.
  I wrongly suspected, do accept my regrets.

That separation like the ashes of cigarettes.
  Thanks; you kept my love in heart secrets.

Have you realized! Negligence really hurts.
  To express inner agony that is why I burst.

You faithfully insisted to express your hurts.
  I wrongly suspected, do accept my regrets.

Arrest-

Come in our marriage bond, give your arrest.
    Some courage for the love bond, it comes first.

The days of our loneliness had been so worst.
    Come in our marriage bond, give your arrest.

Honey waiting to receive, you are my life thirst.
    Some courage for the love bond, it comes first.

No more rush, with respect take love life rest.
    Come in our marriage bond; give your arrest.

Soul to the soul, body to the body for the best.
    Some courage for the love bond, it comes first.

Express your emotion; bestow on me your trust.
    Come in our marriage bond, to give your arrest.

No more mission for ambition that idea was worst.
    Show some courage for the love bond comes first.

Angry lover in love fever.

Angry lover thinks you may lose your senses.
In a blink, you filled my heart with offences.

You have been changing, eyes like lenses.
Angry lover thinks you may lose your senses.

This life been in trouble, I paid much expenses.
In a blink you filled my heart with such offences.

Worrying life without you, come I lost my senses.
Street to street and town to town with differences.

Strained by asking in letters to allow some divorces.
Blindly annoyed but thanks for the unseen forces.

Angry lover, angry lover sends some love curses.
Angry lover, angry lover been writing these verses.

Angry lover, angry lover in love fever with crisis.
Love tears, everywhere regular as daily sun rises.

Thinking for linking.

She is thinking; she is linking her love world.
    She is crying; she is trying for her love world.

She is flying in her dreams like love bird.
    She is shining, high flying up above bird.

She is lovely; she is searching in every crowd.
    She is roaming, she is moaning still she proud.

She does mumble; she is humble some time loud.
    She is high, still annoyed up above in the cloud.

She in worry, in much hurry for divine tide.
    She would like in the ferry a love fine ride.

She would like to show her love instead to hide.
    She would like to remove annoyance on her side.

She will learn to remove all burns, she so proud.
    She will earn divine turns, the only one in crowd.

Answer my query?

Come, answer my queries don't blame me.
  Come my Mary just in heart en-frame me.

No more delay, allow to distain me.
  Answer my query do not blame me.

My love you just officially name me.
  Come, my Mary just en-frame me.

I want access to you, do not refrain me.
  Please, answer my query do not blame me.

Love, listen my story to maintain me.
  Come my Mary in heart en-frame me.

Please, do not show anger to abstain me.
  Come, answer my query, do not blame me.

I been crying, I been trying do not detain me.
  I have heard, come my Mary just en-frame me.

<u>Respect.</u>

Respect my dealing do not give me a scratch.
Accept my feeling do not give me a speech.

Are you responsible for the delay of our reach?
Respect my dealing; do not give me a scratch.

My love has been yours, avoiding any breech.
Accept my feeling do not give me a speech.

Have you seen the beats of my heart in patch?
Respect my dealing do not give me a speech.

Yes I can't afford that my love to be snatched.
Accept my feelings do not give me a speech.

O, love! Do you think love needs to be preached?
Respect my dealing do not give me a scratch.

Have a little think my love, I always been in your reach.
Please; do accept my feelings, do not give a speech.

Response.

I have been a hunt of your changing response.
　　I have been waiting to see your caring glance.

Yes, I do remember your tears with silent romance.
　　But I have been a hunt of your changing response.

I been around you, we lost a chance after chance.
　　I have been waiting to see your great caring glance.

Come to fly, do not deny you are my life substance.
　　Yes, I have been a hunt of your changing response.

Come to move, come to live, avail this brilliant chance.
　　Always I have been waiting to see your caring glance.

Come to cut all distance, O you my vital substance.
　　However, I been a hunt of your changing response.

Don't you know, don't you know, love your romance.
　　Come to me, hum to me; heal my pains with your glance.

Why not today, why not to day, do not lose this chance.
　　Do you believe, I been a hunt of your changing response.

<u>My Thirsty Heart.</u>

Would you give a divine drink through your lips?
    Really it is sweeter than honey, I want more sips.

No excuses for delay and do not play any tricks.
    Please, give me a divine drink through your lips.

Yours rosy lips, thirsty heart wants more sips.
    Give me your loving smile, to keep me relax.

Keep your arms around me, this broken heart to fix.
    Would you give me a divine drink through your lips?

First drown yourself in love, this broken heart to fix.
    Infact, some little, little things cause true lovers splits.

Do not forget in real life humbleness attracts.
    Don't you feel to flourish these dieing ethics?

Cure my hurts including all love given pricks.
    Would you favor my efforts to get back relax?

Let me expose the spark in chest through my texts.
    I hungry for your company, update your contacts.

Separation caring botheration, no more complexes.
    Situations were worst by playing those wrong tricks.

So much depress, need a drink through your lips.
    Express whatever you suggest, to link more sips.

Give your attention.

Now explore my heart and give your attention.
     Ignore that delay, remove any growing tension.

Sign that marriage contract with true conviction.
     Now explore my heart and give your attention.

You are the one living in my heart's love section.
     Ignore that delay, remove any growing tension.

Behave like lover, to increase your attraction.
     Now explore my heart and give your attention.

Reality is here our life is more than a fiction.
     Ignore that delay, remove any growing tension.

Years, years wait as you my love life selection.
     Now explore my heart and give your attention.

You have seen, you have heard, you are exception.
     To ignore that delay, remove any growing tension.

Oh my rare, rare wife, forgive any life friction.
     Now explore my heart and give your attention.

Pleasant days and nights, in your way my affection.
     Your innocent reply, you are my soul love perfection.

Lover Hunger.

Dreadful days and nights, I want to be with you.
       Terrible sights, still don't you know! I love you.

It is hunger for you, don't think it is diet! I miss you.
       Yes this love is like a ringer, now I want to kiss you.

Don't deny, don't deny! Come to bless, I miss you.
       You are like a dream on the sky, nevertheless but you.

Whatever I ever enjoy, I want to share with you.
       Here and there your sighs, now I do care of you.

Our bodies are away but this soul is very near to you.
       Then to suspend between us that annoy, fly with you.

Whatever I have told that is true, no more lie to you.
       Now to express and prove, I am no more, shy to you.

This youth is melting; I am asking, where are you?
       Yes, I have been wondering in your love to find you.

You, the only one.

Let us honey, have love's legal life with fun.
    Really, you have been my desire the only one.

I do remember those clothing, garden and run.
    Let us honey, to have love legal life with fun.

Someone saw my salutation as a firing gun.
    Really, you have been my desire the only one.

At your door, that response made me stunned.
    Let us honey, have love's legal life with fun.

Since seven years time what you have learned.
    Really, you have been my desire the only one.

Come to explore, what in your love I have done.
    Let us honey, to have love legal life with fun.

Dear wife, O my life; all complaints to be shunned.
    Do you know you have been my desire the only one?

Fairy Lady.

You are the holly ever fairy lady of my fortune.
   On the bright skies of love, you are my moon.

Oh, my jewellery, are you diamond or ruby stone.
   You are the holly ever fairy lady of my fortune.

You are hanging as necklace on my chest all alone.
   Yes, on the bright skies of love, you are my moon.

Not only love, you are also my flesh and bone.
   You are the holly ever fairy lady of my fortune.

Good bye to delay, now receive me very soon.
   On the bright skies of love, you are my moon.

In the Garden of expression you are the love tune.
   You are the holly ever fairy lady of my fortune.

Since that day the tree of our love has more grown.
   Yes, on the bright skies of love, you are my moon.

Oh, you flower of the flowers, without thorn.
   You are the holly ever fairy lady of my fortune.

Anxiety and Priority.

Worried love, unemployment, just life is in anxiety.
 Losing health, no more wealth, you are my priority.

You are mine, do combine, divine love in a variety.
 Worried love, unemployment, just life is in anxiety.

Now a day true love in the whole world is in minority.
 Losing health, no more wealth, you are my priority.

You have a God gifted love, don't chase curiosity.
 Worried love, unemployment, just life is in anxiety.

Unknowingly, some one has been wasted generosity.
 Losing health, no more wealth, you are my priority.

Yet, many chances are there, to avail that diversity.
 Worried love, unemployment, just life is in anxiety.

Few measures can restore that interval in prosperity.
 Losing health, no more wealth, you are my priority.

Why worry! Once you marry; overcome this society.
 This worried love, unemployment, just life is in anxiety.

On Love Flames.

Since then on love flames, I am burning,
    See my grieved heart, life is just turning.

Unaware, now youth is something learning,
    Since then on love flames, I am burning.

Message after message, she is not confirming,
    You, see my grieved heart, life is just turning.

Your shadow all around is now returning,
    Since then on love flames, I am burning.

With a hope I do cope for next morning,
    See my grieved heart, life is just turning.

Silence and negligence are getting boring,
    Since then on love flames, I am burning.

Love expression, truth and reality are scoring,
    Honey see my grieved heart, life is just turning.

With knowledge, experience, life is forming,
    And since then on love flames, I am burning.

Would you forgive this lover, o my darling?
    You, see my grieved heart, life is just turning.

Don't suspect my intention

Love, I am staying in your paths, want your attention,
    Praying for your love, you don't suspect my intention.

Love is tender like petals, do not give harsh re-action,
    Love, I am staying in your paths, want your attention.

Loss of love, loss of jobs, life is full with this tension,
    Praying for your love, you don't suspect my intention.

Life is jammed with the traffic of suspicion's junction,
    Love, I am staying in your paths, want your attention.

Cruel hurdles of your customs, now in need of action,
    Praying for your love, you don't suspect my intention.

Heart control's our life with its large cordial section,
    Love, I am staying in your paths, want your attention.

World is wide but this heart bide by your attraction,
    Praying for your love, you don't suspect my intention.

Glade tidings for the faithful, next life is extension,
    Love, I am staying in your paths, want your attention.

Don't conceal your love, to avoid future life eruption,
    Praying for your love, you don't suspect my intention.

I still remember that girl.

I was travelling from another town to see someone in airport,
  While thinking, in waiting lounge she was holding her passport.

Time was tight so I arranged a couple of bouquet in love support,
  She was called back from waiting lounge with my arrival report.

Wearing blue dress, a glass was between us, like in love court,
  Within silence, I presented those flowers with hi from my throat.

She was looking in my eyes, her father then provided us support,
  She was annoyed in her heart what caused such a delay in his route.

Still I remember that little girl, while standing in that airport,
  Several hours journey but her questioning looks were its fruit.

That take off of the plane in my life was one of the cruellest abort,
  Those couple bunches, one for her father and the other for love root.

Until now, somebody never said a word in my thirsty heart court,
  I have been very stress that she never sent forward her love report.

In the city of my heart.

Honey, you are cute in the heart of my city,
    You would be proud to call you my pretty.

In my life, you are embodied nicely natty,
    Honey, you are cute in the heart of my city.

To emerge our life in a sense loving pity,
    You would be proud to call you my pretty.

Goodbye to misunderstanding without ratty,
    Honey, you are cute in the heart of my city.

Restoration for the past, in future to be witty,
    You would be so proud to call you my pretty.

Stuffy days are gone, now some are gritty,
    Honey, you are cute in the heart of my city.

Ferry of suspicion, to be docked in love jetty,
    You would be so proud to call you my pretty.

Without you in every step, my life was empty,
    As soon we restored our lives, joy will be plenty.

Are You? -

Have you heard that buzz of my soul to you?
    Have you felt that craze of my soul for you?

Apart from dreams, this poetry is a think of you,
    Apart from the screams, my heart is a link of you.

You have been my desire; life is unfulfilled without you,
    Life has been like hell, many years like on fire without you.

Your attention has been missing, life a tension without you,
    That early departure has been ambition, such treason of you.

Those letters with your response have been diversion from you,
    A heart full of love has been turned, like a surgeon for you.

Once you hurt your love, life has been incomplete without you,
    Again never misunderstand my love, o perfect wife; I love you.

Dear Life Partner?

Oh dear life partner, you are my rose petal, rose petal,
    For my entire mistake in love, I do feel very little, little.

Since the day no one but you been so much vital, so vital,
    Oh dear life partner, you are my rose petal, rose petal.

Read my report then give your support to settle, settle,
    For my entire mistake in love, I do feel very little, little.

In separation, annoyed feelings were like battle, battle,
    Oh dear life partner, you are my rose petal, rose petal.

Have a dream life and each moment, be a twinkle, twinkle,
    For my entire mistake in love, I do feel very little, little.

Wish our lives so delicious with a flavour of pickle, pickle,
    Oh dear life partner, you are my rose petal, rose petal.

You should know, the Khaperai is your given title, title,
    For my entire mistake in love, I do feel very little, little.

Alone but not insane but in your view I was mental, mental,
    My love, you my blood, your's origin is my national, national.

The Happiest or Heaviest day?

The happiest time of my life was the day of our marriage,
  The heaviest time was the day, when you broke my courage.

My body, soul was amused, as you reached to my village,
  The happiest time of my life was the day of our marriage.

A word tragedy with tears, my heart drowned in that drainage,
  The heaviest time was the day, when you broke my courage.

Truly I tried many attempts, to reassure and encourage,
  The happiest time of my life was the day of our marriage.

Until now, my heart, mind is still yours love carriage,
  The heaviest time was the day, when you broke my courage.

With few words life get destroy, like brain hammerage,
  The happiest time of my life was the day of our marriage.

Oh, my love, you are my life, my home and my luggage,
  The heaviest time was the day, when you broke my courage.

When we married on that day was so proud our village,
  The happiest time of my life was the day of our marriage.

Broken Glass.

Why you can't see my heart is like a broken glass,
   Because of you, in my life profit turned to real loss.

Before life garden been full of colour and green grass,
   Why you can not see my heart is like a broken glass.

Who did turn! Our love life like a frozen frost,
   Because of you in my life, profit turned in loss.

My heart beats in your love garden which I never did cross,
   Why you then can not see my heart is like a broken glass.

I been angry and yours love hungry, O my boss,
   Because of you in my life profit turned in loss.

One to one you never believed, now singing within mass,
   Why you then can not see, my heart is like a broken glass.

Would you agree! You did not answer my love toss,
   Because of you, in my life profit turned in real loss.

Being in the same house, the distance was like earth and Mars,
   O, love then why you can't see my heart is like a broken glass.

This World is not a place for love!

She said; this world is not a place for our love,
   He says love come to my lap to fly like dove.

We will meet in paradise then I will see my love,
   Don't get pathetic, tears from the eyes to remove.

I was living like psychic, if you true then why you did not prove,
   I was confused in my thinking; now my confidence will grow.

For years, I have been all alone in my home that is true,
   Even in anger, I kept yours belonging, I did not throw.

Anguish within us, still hope to get back I did not reprove,
   Alas! When we were together like bad weather life screw.

I don't know why! You tried to reconcile but I was in rave,
   You have been in front of my eyes; my room was like cave.

A thought but that idea was blank, that I will live like slave,
   In my heart I was offended; why you did not keep clean shave?

Fine, fine, O mine; a mistake that you did not realize burning love,
   I rather say, forgive about last, now come to fly like divine dove.

BAD DAYS ARE GONE.

Bad days are gone, come to pick your share,
    Enjoy your love life, come to track our care.

No suspicion, create good impression O dear,
    Bad days are gone, come to pick your share.

Believe me! You have been to me very near,
    Enjoy your love life, come to track our care.

Hope on the horizon, I do witness to bear,
    Bad days are gone, come to pick your share.

Room in my heart, for you always been spare,
    Enjoy your love life, come to track our care.

Yours heavy heart and I feel your love tear,
    Bad days are gone, come to pick your share.

You have proved; you are true that is clear,
    Enjoy your love life, come to track our care.

Remember; I came to your door step very near?
    Bad days are gone, come to pick your share.

Then you broke into a run, did you sense some fear?
    Love, enjoy your love life, come to track our care.

In This Crowded World.

You and me, come to fly oh my loving bird,
    This heart beat's for you, she has never heard.

You the only divine asset of my loving world,
    This heart beat's for you, she has never heard.

A tribute, pay attention to my singing word,
    You and me, come to fly oh my loving bird.

Then come to live around like a grazing herd,
    You and me, come to fly oh my loving bird.

Why we so much lonely in this crowded world,
    This heart beat's for you, she has never heard.

You in dreams like a white dove and a singing bird,
    Why not you and me come to fly oh my loving bird.

Your concern in my life has been wide spread,
    God know's in your love this heart has gone red.

Consider my worry

Listen O you cruel heart, to consider my worry?
      Otherwise, you will find my dead body to burry.

Why you did not see my love oh dear fairy?
      Check your love in my heart, it does carry.

Our loss of youth, time is gone in such hurry,
      O, beloved I remember that plans to get marry.

Days and nights are gone, you tell me love theory,
      Remove burdens from your heart with love bravery.

Fine, expectations and complaints are not a pillory,
      The best earning of this life, as you are my salary.

You are in large within life, since the day we did marry,
      Come accept my truth then all complaints need to burry.

Majority of Politicians.

You all cunning and shameless politicians good bye,
     Hellfire is awaiting, nobody will listen to your cry.

You do anything for power and keep telling lie,
     After losing your office, you seem such ugly spy.

While in office you are crushing humanity in one try,
     Bloodshed but your fake smile and eyes never shy.

Oh, cousins of the devils that blood shed would you deny?
     God has no mercy for you; your hearts are dark and very dry.

When devil asks for worship, you are the first to apply,
     You have deprived generations of guidance to supply.

Yours legislations and constitutions are almost evil ally,
     You have left, such a Will to your children, to God deny!

You will lose everything and tomorrow you will die,
     Yours slogans for the best interest never end as you lie.

It is all about you.

The warm feelings in my heart are all about you,
    The one who makes my dreams restless that is you.

The happiest days of life were all around you,
    Love, I am proud of my singing song about you.

That silence of years, these words tell about you,
    The love accompanied me in loneliness that is you.

Do not ignore my concern always think about you,
    Do restore my trust; all worries do come about you.

That real place in my heart is still empty for you,
    Do you know this heart is still livening city of you?

Hate and love both dwell combine to find you,
    Love will surround to expel anguish about you.

Am I not true! Then to approve that is only you,
    Some complaints but true love survives about you.

<u>Some Time.-</u>

Then I am young; I am old in my feelings,
    Yes I am kind; I am cruel in my dealings.

Some time fake, some time real in my screaming,
    Some time happy, some time heavy in dreaming.

Some time silent, some time reactive to other blaming,
    Some time possessive, some time expressive in sailings.

Some time beauty but not a show piece, fancy veiling,
    Some time forgiveness, some time harsh for healings.

Some time wrong, some time find the cause of stealing,
    Some time punishment, some time cage with its railings.

Some time neglect, some time listen to people appealing,
    Some time tired some time pride in my helping roaming.

Some time money, some time with pocket runny mailings,
    Some time here, some time there for past fixing dealings.

DON'T TOUCH.

I hate you, I hate you, don't touch,
　　　You are late, you are late so much.

I Waite you, I Waite you don't rush!
　　　I love you, I love you don't blush!

Engrave me, engrave in heart sketch,
　　　Don't be that cruel, cruel that much.

Petrol me, control me get love clutch,
　　　You a cure for my broken heart stitch.

Contact me, contact me; keep switch,
　　　So sweet, so sweet each loving touch.

Sorry, if you see any offence!

Love, I am sorry, if you have seen any offence,
    As for I know; my heart has been your entrance.

To me separation is the worst ever paid expense,
    Love, I am sorry, if you have seen any offence.

Keep one to one discussion to avoid life dense,
    As for I know; my heart has been your entrance.

Concealing your love in heart is out of sense,
    Love, I am sorry, if you have seen any offence.

Don't be blind to allow for love such distance,
    As for I know; my heart has been your entrance.

Days of life are on count down with your silence,
    As for I know; my heart has been your entrance.

With out you the tune of life has gone un-balanced,
    As for I know; my heart has been your entrance.

Fairy, I never ever mean to make our life tense,
    As for I know; my heart has been your entrance.

Do you remember, my love mentioned sentence?
    As for I know; my heart has been your entrance.

Away from you; still keeping your remembrance,
    As for I know; my heart has been your entrance.

You are the one to bring back our life sequence,
    As for I know; my heart has been your entrance.

Garden Four

<u>Jesus.</u>

Your mild disposition faced such wild opposition oh beloved Jesus,
      Blessed was your mother, you are loved in the heart of our pieces.

Your birth was a miracle, but those devils filled horrendous cases,
      Blessed was your mother, you are loved in the heart of our pieces.

Satan's were around you; eventually you were raised above spaces,
      Your mild disposition faced such wild opposition oh beloved Jesus.

In your worldly life, you were tortured verbally by those evil races,
      Blessed was your mother, you are loved in the heart of our pieces.

On your mother, God has bestowed His blessing from divine bases,
      Your mild disposition faced such wild opposition oh beloved Jesus.

None of them were listening to you; they had always tow faces,
      Blessed was your mother, you are loved in the heart of our pieces.

In your time, true Christians were in Europe, they truly did embrace,
      Your mild disposition faced such wild opposition oh beloved Jesus.

Not only Mary they always tortured prophets as loose are their laces,
      Blessed was your mother, you are loved in the heart of our pieces.

Oh Jesus don't get upset, we love you all with your best praises,
      Your mild disposition faced such wild opposition oh beloved Jesus.

Grand Father.

O, grandfather, you are a strong tree of German so calm,
    The Angel has given to us your name Abdul-Salaam.

Be the blessing and mercy upon you with calm, calm,
    O, grandfather, you are a strong tree of German so calm.

I saw your blessed face on the heavens with charm,
    The Angel has given to us your name Abdul-Salaam.

You left the lands of German by divine Ilham, Ilham,
    O, grandfather, you are a strong tree of German so calm.

Yours lovely grey beard, been living in Afghanistan,
    The Angel has given to us your name Abdul-Salaam.

As you touched the lands of Afghanistan, skies presented salaam,
    O, dear grandfather, you are a strong tree of German so calm.

The German lands with tears but Afghanistan was balm and balm,
    The Angel has given to us your name, Abdul-salaam, Abdul-salaam.

O, dear and near servant of Allah, I am sending my salaam, salaam.
    O, grandfather, you are a strong tree of Afghanistan and Alman.

WE LOVE TREES.

Many grown up trees are bringing so much fruit,
  We do not think they are sweetening our throat.

We just use then abuse, all careless of its root,
  Trees give greenery, nice scenery and also fruit.

Much with flowers, shading cover, a cooling coat,
  It provides woods with much patience to facilitate.

Let us, grow more trees it also needs our treat,
  Say good words to the trees to remove their fret.

We love trees, trees love us green world to create,
  We are free to grow more trees, enjoy so much fruit.

Your shadow, in autumn you live like widow in a threat,
  We are selfish, cutting your life, so sorry for rude treat.

This furniture, you so good by nature, in towns Street,
  Ambition for the year; woods, fruit, shade without retreat.

ANIMALS.

Animals do efforts to satisfy their hunger need,
  Faithful to the owner, they just want to be fed.

They want good treatment in life to be pleased,
  If you deal wrongly, they desire to be released.

No doubt, they are fighting to fulfil their greed,
  Selfish men use them for money gamble speed.

They are carrying various natures in their seed,
  They also take interest to continue their breed.

Many are wild, in cage they are tired, want to be freed,
  They want their natural life; men are stopping to succeed.

Some carry poison but never attack, if not teased,
  Some are monsters if come across we get freeze.

We think often, why so many animals have been breed?
  They may say why so much men, women, they not agreed.

Animals enjoy only this world; to Hellfire they never lead,
  Jinn and Men are obliged for their clear actions to be freed.

Eagles in the heaven-

In a dream I saw many Eagles in a row like soldier,
     On the side a mountain, covered with Eagles in order.

As I landed all of them opened their wings in an order,
     In a dream I saw many Eagles in a row like soldier.

Touching sight with great number made me wonder,
     On the side a mountain, covered with Eagles in order.

That mountain filled with Eagles, they were bolder,
     In a dream I saw many Eagles in a row like soldier.

He took me to a blessed place, for a food in corridor,
     On the side a mountain, covered with Eagles in order.

I was a guest; the host was kind, nice and prouder,
     In a dream I saw many Eagles in a row like soldier.

After a long time three of them landed in a splendor,
     Unfortunately, they were fighting, it was a blunder.

That is why I fired a bullet towards that offender,
     Except the third Eagle, the tow escaped to surrender.

Anyway, the blessed Eagles of the Lord as a reminder,
     The creation of the Lord and their qualities are wider.

Why Mistake about Angels-

A blessed creation of the Lord, having wings they can fly,
  The Arch Angels carrying a size from the earth to the sky.

One pair of wings to the several hundreds they live in the sky,
  A blessed creation of the Lord, all having wings they can fly.

The oldest creation in the Universe, in this world they never die,
  The Arch Angels carrying a massive size from the earth to sky.

They can speak any language of the world; they are not shy,
  A blessed creation of the Lord, all having wings they can fly.

They are the trustworthy, powerful and lighted creation very high,
  The Arch Angels carrying a massive size from the earth to the sky.

The length of the one pair wings Angel reaches thousands feet high,
  A blessed creation of the Lord, all having wings anywhere they can fly.

The Angels, Jibreal, Mikeal, Israfeal, Izraeal, Mlaik; can you deny?
  The Arch Angels carrying a massive size from the earth, to the sky.

Mankind and Jin cannot see the Angels, because of their eye,
  A blessed creation of the Lord, all having wings they can fly.

They are kind; they are wise to glorify our Lord very high,
 The Arch Angels carrying a size from the earth, to the sky.

They are handling a huge task, every day without any annoy,
 A blessed creation of the Lord, all having wings they can fly.

They can sort out devils in a blink but wait for the command high,
 The Arch Angels carrying a massive size from the earth, to sky.

In the first sky of the stars, they shower stars fire on the spy,
 A blessed creation of the Lord, all having wings they can fly.

Such a shame some fools see the Angels like fairies in their eye,
 The Arch Angels carrying a massive size from the earth to sky.

Why people do mistake to understand the archaeological signs bye,
 In the past, rebellious nations had been upside down in your history.

Never carry worldly desire, relations like Jin and men in their body,
 A blessed creation of the Lord, having wings anywhere they can fly.

Salutations to the Angels, with such excellence they do cry,
 The Arch Angels really carrying a massive size up in the sky.

That evening in the village.

Calm life in the village, there some flowers of the daffodils,
    Those farmers were working in the fields by that village hills.

Young children were playing in the sand by that water mill,
    Calm life in the village, there some flowers of the daffodils.

Other youngsters were grazing cattle and plying routine drill,
    Those farmers were working in the fields by that village hills.

Some girls were making paper boats without any paddles,
    Calm life in the village, there some flowers of the daffodils.

By the village front, I saw boys were playing football very well,
    Those farmers were working in the fields by that village hills.

In the upper skirt, fruits garden were loaded with nice smell,
    Calm life in the village, there some flowers of the daffodils.

Pleasant noise from the river, it was flowing with no hurdle,
    Those farmers were working in the fields by that village hills.

On the shoulders of farmers they were carrying grass bundle,
    Calm life in the village, there some flowers of the daffodils.

Many boys were swimming in the fresh canal like fishing drill,
    Those farmers were working in the fields by that village hills.

Many busy in the gossip, by the roadside in the evening still,
    Calm life in the village, there some flowers of the daffodils.

Oh, village I remember that pleasant breeze like heavens lull,
    Those farmers were working in the fields by that village hills.

Do you know why?

People are anxious everywhere do you know, why?
    Many are suffering in a number, do you know why?

Everybody is confused, what will happen do you know why?
    So many marriages are breaking around, do you know why?

Everybody, runs in greed, to gain some more, do you know why?
    Everybody trusts and peace of mind is gone, do you know why?

Look all the time blood shedding is going on, do you know why?
    Though, totally wrong, still claim to be right, do you know why?

Everything is artificial, reality is gone, and do you know why?
    Family systems, morals are upside down, do you know why?

Listen to the recipe with a condition to why? You must apply.
    O, dear, whatever misled you, that dark completely to deny?

Do not follow blindly, what you hear from a spy,
    Prefer the hereafter, instead of this world hi-fie.

Extinguish the zeal of greed, which creates annoy,
    Be mindful, whatever you do is watched from the sky.

Crush all mischief and temptations now go high,
    What satisfies your soul, open your heart eye?

Come to Allah, you brother, sister, that is to apply,
    O, father and mother, be a believer, do not be shy.

Flying Thoughts.

In the universe, my thoughts are everywhere flying,
    Like a flying bird, my thoughts are high surviving.

My thought comes across with a deal interesting,
    Searching around is there anything with trusting.

A wonderful thing, no boundary in a wandering,
    In a minute crossing the whole world unseen gardening.

My thoughts looking for you and to you speaking,
    Where ever go for your lovely glances are seeking.

Some thoughts bring action, while body is sleeping,
    Re-action of the soul in a dream causes pleasing.

Some thoughts go side by side while dreaming,
    Thoughts represent your elf in a real roaming.

Thoughts and heart resemble like body and breathing,
    Love the one connects heart and soul as you believing.

Your thoughts reflect you, in that daily dealing,
    Be cautious about as your thoughts are leading.

Thoughts tell what your inner self proceeding,
    Ill thoughts are like in real from others steeling.

<u>True Dream.</u>

True dreams are those, which comes tomorrow in real,
    You are one of the dreams, which came to me in real.

What has made you so pathetic to have hurt feel?
    You are one of the dreams, which came to me in real.

No more pains in love be together, like a spring of heal,
    True dream are those, which comes tomorrow in real.

No mistrust, no suspect, blessing starts with zeal,
    You are one of dream, which came to me in real.

Please, realize that you are a part of my body and soul,
    True dreams are those, which comes tomorrow in real.

Accept this union, oh the Owner of body and soul,
    You are one of the dreams, which came to me in real.

My thanks, for giving innocent heart, with a true deal,
    Get astonished, to find such a high place in mind, soul.

True drams are those, which come tomorrow in real,
    You are one of the dreams, which came to me in real.

Be The Angels Around You.

Be the blessed Angels around you,
     My body and soul say I love you.

Ringing bells of heart ring about you,
     Be the blessings of God all surround you.

The blessed Jin girls raise their concern about you,
     Any innocent may never suffer in love like you.

The wisdom of lover may grow about you,
     I wish, may the help of God shower on you.

My mistakes in some way need to be improved,
     The kindness of God may also improve you.

Love is tender; no one may suffer as I do,
     Without limit is this bond really for you.

Sorry, I went blunt by that love in years row,
     Bow to God with love is better than other bow.

Literature.

Literature does inspire but you must take its best,
    Say no to the evil; check what you find in its zest.

Think positive, absorb the truth and leave the rest,
    Don't approve crime promotion and vulgar worst.

Have a deep breath, no idea to impose if you trust,
    True love with in its limits, other abuses need arrest.

Brother and sisters spread the good like speedy gust,
    You are civilized, not sex slaves as controlled by lust.

The western world has its qualities, why now in dust?
    You are children of Noah, David; now like iron in rust.

Where are you heading! Don't you feel pain in your chest?
    What in your poetry, novels and drama, like shameful lust.

Think for a while, after death each soul get strong arrest,
    Fine if Paradise but hard and very hot is Hellfire thirst.

So called Healers?

Subdue and discipline your lover as you wish,
 Inspect and react at your home, ask to brush.

Pretend you are so angry but avoid any push,
 Give impression you need not lover like bush.

Tell that many asked for your hand, you are not a fish,
 Show your ambitions; that life is not only to cook dish.

Explain you are not too bad, to cook potato mash,
 That is I don't suggest you to cause marriage crash.

Why you never reminded my beauty, Mum praise eyes lash,
 Further my family of such status to invite you with any clash.

Tell, I am independent, need not your support and any cash,
 Don't worry, if you cry each night, he will also get smash.

The end ruins you, magicians ask for more money splash,
 I say get a gun; kill all this spread evil to the Hell fire trash.

West under evil with secular agenda, sinking divorces blush,
 Social life and families are broken with such increasing rush.

Can you see the difference?

Ha, can you see on the sky that relaxing lights,
  I can feel very deep that attractive loving gaits.

Can you find something bright on the heights?
  I can feel very deep that attractive loving gaits.

Around on the earth, can you see Angel's flights?
  Ha, ha, can you see on the sky that relaxing lights.

Have you ever seen, any Angels with a might,
  I can feel very deep that attractive loving gaits.

Dark, light is the difference within days and nights,
  Ha, ha, can you see on the sky that relaxing lights.

Have you ever seen in a dream divine sights?
  I can feel very deep that attractive loving gaits.

Can you see the difference within lefts and rights?
  Ha, ha, can you see on the sky that relaxing lights.

Can you see, difference between peace and fights,
  Then, I can feel very deep that attractive loving gaits.

Gosh, Josh and Ghosts.

Weeping ghosts said we are drowning in our own astrology,
  We are worst in religion but we are good in new technology.

Further, bad fortune is going on we are losing our psychology,
  Weeping ghosts said we are drowning in our own astrology.

Then what about us! Pharaoh has left behind only archeology,
  We are worst in religion but we are good in new technology.

Once ago God has changed our ancestors with bad biology,
  Weeping ghosts said we are drowning in our own astrology.

Regardless of any results, we never ask for defeated apology,
  We are worst in religion but we are good in new technology.

Cleverness, girls and the use of wealth is our old ideology,
  Weeping ghosts said we are drowning in our own astrology.

Our politicians and agencies know to use media terminology,
  We are worst in religion but we are good in new technology.

Astrology is our hidden religion and we believe in technology,
  Then what about us! Pharaoh has left behind only archeology.

Jinns conversation.

We have seen, fine real poetry in our own history,
    We understand life chemistry by true missionary.

From every wrong belief, we want to be free,
    With true faith, we have very fresh memory.

Now, we do not say to God; One, Tow, Three,
    Our past actions in life have given us so worry.

Thanks to God, the devil will have no more any country,
    Thus to change to the truth, everybody has so much hurry.

We will keep the life on the true path, extra-ordinary,
    To fallow the commands of Allah, are too compulsory.

Alas, our lives in the past have been so derogatory,
    Now we know, what is true what is wrong literally.

O friends, true faith needs its own directory,
    No more in the dark, now we got true entry.

Yes, no more incline to the devils laboratory,
    A peace of mind is with Islam, true serenity.

<u>Happy birthday to you.</u>

Oh my love I really miss you, miss you,
    Come to me, I may kiss you; kiss you.

Happy birthday, all the best I wish you,
    Oh my love I really miss you, miss you.

Be your life in blessing that I wish you,
    Come to me I may kiss you; kiss you.

Every pleasant moment, I may assess you,
    My love, don't you know, I badly miss you.

Lovely flowers in your way I wish you,
    Come to me, I may kiss you; kiss you.

Thanks for love, you are above, I do miss you,
    I wish you may get in life whatever impresses you.

Happy birthday to you, all the time I miss you,
    May Allah, fulfill your entire wish, I wish you.

132

Few corners of the cities.

Now a day, every day's stories in the cities of the world is a stress,
    Watching and reading the media is showing all sinister reverse.

Un-employment, safety concern, measures are very less and less,
    War on terror has taken more innocent lives in disgrace like curse.

Protest, processions in the streets of cities then shouting address,
    Peace lovers' hearts are heavy with this entire war surplus, surplus.

Stormed cities with bloodshed and politicians' agenda express,
    Evil agenda lies and other people lives are like flies without bless.

In cities people have abandoned religions because of media and press,
    Everybody has a run, to have earned for their daily burn, more
    or less.

Daily news of paedophiles, many politicians' crocodile with policy harass,
    Evil policy's effects on other nations are failing; without to do
    impress.

In the cities and towns, how many get drown their lives just meaningless,
    Now a days, treacherous, liars, and blunt agents are every where
    famous.

Tragedy of Religions.

In theory every one claims that they are on the true religion,
    Alas! When we come to the truth, they lack God's vision.

Many combine astrology with their home made religion,
    What a pity! They have made it a source of their provision.

Few of them were familiar with Scriptures but they created a division,
    Jealousy, prejudice and stubbornness have caused a failure in
    large region.

Then what a fuss! Every one claims, one God in their worst treason,
    In wrong belief, once you die then who can save from Hellfire prison.

Every day and night is a blank paper; you are the writer of your action,
    Remember, once you see the death then the mercy never get
    attraction.

God is not in need of anyone, this life is a test for next selection,
    Definitely, Paradise and Hellfire is the place, one has to earn.

God is mercy, God is blessing, and God is love we often mention,
    Also God is wrath for the evil; God is force without any emotion.

Have a glimpse on the nation's history, Prophets Nations and their location,
    After long time patience from heavens, now the Angels need an
    action.

Then What?

Suppose I become a politician of the world, then what?
    If, I take a charge as a General, have the world, then what?

In case I become the richest man of the world, then what?
    Then I practice my life as scholar of the world, then what?

Suppose I become a supper sports man of the world, then what?
    If I collecting the lives and deaths of the world in my fest; then what?

In case I remove all devils from the earth by sword, then what?
    Then I walk and fly with Angels like a divine bird, then what?

Nevertheless, I get all miracles from the Lord right now, then what?
    Then bring blessing and stressing around the whole world; then what?

A query since childhood what I lost, what I search; don't know yet,
    Anyway, it is certain what I want to be near to the Lord without cut.

SINNER JERK.

Some time think about many people and different work,
    Can you see any difference in a solicitor and office clerk?

Solicitor is a clerk who explains dead books in a work,
    Judge is a sinner who twists the law with easy pen Jerk.

What is the difference between a butcher and a doctor work?
    The butcher charges less and the surgeon charges to the bulk.

What is the difference between a politician and a religious clerk?
    Politicians run for power, fame and the other for unseen silk.

Be good teacher but not a lazy preacher like that jerks,
    Be a farmer but not a harmer to neighbors like lurk.

Religious stubbornness and negligence have taken our mark,
    Race of money with greed brings in us so much evil stark.

Then by the end we see our life really dark,
    Who would like to be self killer then embark?

God loves humbleness.

I don't know why people get in old age so fate?
    O sweetie, think today about before it is too late.

I don't say to be a skinny, this matter is delicate,
    Invitation for a lunch means a lunch, not a date!

Who can be perfect yet better to get conversate?
    Honey, my love has been for you in heart plate.

The links and signals always been very straight,
    Concerns have been truly original in each debate.

My heart is already with then what for to wait?
    True love is my treasure, don't care for house and flat.

Why somebody is deep to hear this Garden vibrate,
    Years in dark were chosen by somebody to isolate.

Why not to sooth sorrows rather than to escalate?
    My soul searches for, as you have been nominated.

I am still young in my love with fresh climate;
    God is pleased with lowered head in a prostrate.

I am not a Machine!

I am not a machine to work all the time!
    I want pleasant social life with extra time.

I am strong enough, don't need beer and wine!
    I do enjoy spending money with family to dine.

Bad fellows are the same, like out of date coin,
    It becomes useless unless to sell as antique sign.

Once you re-gain broken hearts that is like anodyne,
    The one who shows loyalty, respect is really sublime.

That haughtiness has pushed many lives now confined,
    Alas! Few are the winner in a way to get re-combined.

Freedom does not mean to violate the borderline,
    Jen and human lives have purpose, with certain design.

Selfish approach in your life is nothing but a bovine,
    If no morals and honesty then body is without spine.

Everybody.

Let us get free from this every day trouble,
   Love is more sensitive than a water bubble.

Let us find peace, an end to the battle,
   Let us talk about matters to get settle.

Take measures for improvement, don't feel little,
   The ways of life need for the best some re-shuffle.

Selfish approaches always cause results very fatal,
   Expectations in real life are more than grazing cattle.

How a fiancée is pleased with ring of gold or mettle,
   Apology to a partner is the same ritual like devils on fable.

Parents should know that children care is more vital,
   Broken partners give their children feelings suicidal.

Oh parents your children learn from you even in the cradle,
   Parent's attitude reflects on children, so avoid bad tackle.

A Soul on the Village Path.

I saw a young walking soul on the village path,
    He was cursing and asking for Allah's wrath.

He said Allah; give to the devils a fire bath,
    I saw a young walking soul on the village path.

Walking with Angels, words from his mouth,
    He was cursing and asking for Allah's wrath.

He with heavy heart he was a loving moth,
    I saw a young walking soul the village path.

He was praising his Lord on the zenith and earth,
    He was walking and asking for Allah's wrath.

He was a blessed soul up in the heavens lofts,
    I saw a young walking soul on the village path.

A divine cup he was sipping a tasty holy broth,
    He was cursing and asking for Allah's wrath.

Until his youth time, revenge he never sought,
    I saw a young walking soul on the village path.

Many Jens were waiting to say hello to the moth,
    Since his childhood he has been in the blessing bath.

By the village water mill he was walking wearing blue cloth,
    Then he was seen by the river, walking to his village path.

He likes play grounds and his village mosque,
    I saw a young walking soul on the village path.

Because I hate!

I wish everybody prosperous because I hate poverty,
    I really wish everybody nice because I hate cruelty.

I wish everybody to be upright because I hate ambiguity,
    I wish everybody success because I hate failing difficulty.

I wish everybody friendly because I hate enmity,
    I wish everybody in peace because I hate atrocity.

I wish everybody keen in love because I hate insensibility,
    I wish everybody legal love because I hate ill-eligibility.

I wish everybody justice, because I hate blind amnesty,
    I wish everybody wisdom because I hate kind brutality.

I wish really everybody pious because I hate heinous entity,
    I wish everybody fearless because I hate stressing facility.

I wish everybody careful because I hate ignored eternity,
    I wish everybody humble because I hate annoyed maternity.

I wish everybody faithful because I hate pagan's nationality,
    I wish everybody helpful because I hate selfish personality.

Life and Wife.

If your wife is good, then like a tent in life,
　　If she is bad, then face life time blunt knife.

If to the taste of you, then everything so right,
　　If she turns a miserable sight, then life is tight.

Some count towards, wealth, beauty, say that is wife,
　　I say oh fine but faith with moral has pleasing height.

She also says if husband is bad, then worth to fight,
　　She also complains that he is also like a blunt knife.

Stop, stop complaints, let us make a pleasant life,
　　Trust, respect from heart, to have a pleasant life.

Now, I am happy so happy, oh my dear wife,
　　I do promise, promise, no more worry in life.

Oh, beloved, beloved, husband that is all right,
　　I too promise, promise, to make our life excite.

Keep pouring love from heart through a glance o wife,
　　So, grateful to Allah, He has given me a faithful wife.

In Foreign Lands.

In foreign lands without you every thing is so strange to me,
  Come love, looking for you, have a love exchange with me.

Everybody culture and their asking look so derange to me,
  In foreign lands without you every thing is so strange to me.

You my partner come for lifetime, everything arrange with me,
  Come my love, looking for you, have a love exchange with me.

Being away from me, sounds like cruel revenge on me,
  In foreign lands without you everything so strange to me.

You the one, with a soul and body engage to me,
  Your style and response seem so change to me.

Everything is harmful, as this loneliness damage to me,
  Your love has given such impression and image to me.

Come to stop all this loneliness, speak with high range to me,
  Come love, looking for you, have a love exchange with me.

Every person, every street and town are so strange to me,
  In foreign lands, without you every thing is strange to me.

Don't behave like pagan?

Why your heart is so hard like a pagan?
    You have ruined my life all in sudden.

Most of my feelings you have written,
    The concern of my heart is still hidden.

Why love with bruises had been beaten?
    This family relation is divinely fastened.

We supposed to be one body, what happen?
    Come on earth to me as our souls met in heaven.

In my imaginations life together will be golden,
    This loneliness has affected my soul, like bitten.

That day when you ran away, hopes went flattened,
    Yet the truth of your love has made hopes hearten.

Why years illusion and confusion blurs my vision,
    Enslave me in your love; let us live in our region.

Unconsciously, I have told though in heart I am frightened,
    Loves, whatever you have acknowledged I am enlightened.

All Children.

I love you all good and behaving children,
    Respect your elders to enjoy their affection.

Be keen in your Scholl with more attention,
    Keep brotherhood strong without tension.

Be grateful to your Creator in life junction,
    Once we were the same like yours section.

Avoid greed, cheating; follow honesty mention,
    Once old people were children; now in pension.

Be thankful to parents without restrictions,
    You are also responsible for daily action.

Learn with patience and remember resurrection,
    Life is test; keep away form all evil attraction.

What you think?

You may be thinking, everything is good, I say, no, no.,
As I think of your love without you, life is still so, so.

Why you refuse to re-settle by saying that no, no,
Together, after a long breakdown it is yet, so, so.

In the beginning, you caused irritation with a no, no,
Tears, sorry can not help-up, my life is still so, so.

The wasted time in past has caused wound in life with no,
For so long the childish attitude has caused our life so, so.

Pleasant life has been turned to ruins with a no, no,
Nothing can fill the wounds of heart; life is, so, so.

Love cannot be sold or bought to replace that no, no,
True love cannot be altered once broken; life is so, so.

Heart and soul never forget, once the love gets no, no,
Wealth positions, cannot remove that pains, life is; so.

It is really sad, once your true love is lost with a no, no,
Then every thing is useless with that hurt; life is so, so.

Your love garden is empty with those bad winds of no, no,
Even planting another garden causes to say, life is; so, so.

Burning Fire.

My feeling and thoughts are getting now burning fire,
    Life has been in test, still to fulfill my burning desire.

Some time has been in other towns like loneliness to hire,
    Day by day my feelings, thoughts are getting burning fire.

Turning a stranger like I have broken all relations wire,
    Life has been in test, still to fulfill my burning desire.

Without you, my life has been like puncture tire,
    My feelings and thoughts are getting burning fire.

Love, be yourself in real, I do not approve any liar,
    Life has been in test, still to fulfill burning desire.

Real love has such deadlines which never does expire,
    My feelings and thoughts are getting burning fire.

You come for ever; true love is not a thing to hire,
    Life has been in test, still to fulfill my burning desire.

<u>Departure.</u>

Heart is getting heavy; when from home you take a departure,
    When you are leaving your love and country that is a torture.

Then you miss your streets, friends and your culture,
    Then recall your childhood and some other adventure.

You feel strongly, the values of yours language in other culture,
    Yours emotion in a motion, when you hurt yours own sculpture.

Then you view yours national values as in a disorder,
    About your faith, family you become much inspector.

Once away from your country, you count national factor,
    You got more experience with ideas, to be a good selector.

Our nations have resources; get hunt by other sources disorder,
    We need action to produce development scheme in real order.

You have values important; to the other be supporter,
    Support the truth in your life, be a good words reporter.

Separation was yours violation.

My thirsty soul has been looking for your presence,
Frosty garden is missing to see your appearance.

Love is not about body, rather something immense,
You can feel once you pay for bother love expense.

Love can not be separation from the heart by any distance,
Do you realize lover count's that negligence a big offence?

Your nature also shows some reaction from inheritance,
Heart is not a shopping centre for any better entrance.

Our life's beauty lay's in the marriage eternal romance,
Living like single making our lives more unbalance.

We get hurt, when we follow un-real blind guidance,
The world is like Jungle with broken society evidence.

Oh dear love, some courage to break such a long silence,
To be honest, I have seen this separation as your violence.

Are you fallen in love?

I have fallen in love, you are heavenly suitable,
    I have seen many but you are only compatible.

I am a lover; all your excuses are acceptable,
    To harmonize with my heart, you are capable.

Hold my hand for life time, I am available,
    Yes to consult your parents that is sensible.

All cultural conditions in our way are so terrible,
    Living like singles, this separation is unbearable.

I can see in your character which is notable,
    Now to discover, all our efforts are reliable.

Your looks, your talks and your feelings are beautiful,
    Whatever you have heard from my lips is meaningful.

In my heart and mind your love is flammable,
    I do agree, what you suggest is fairly sensible.

More than numerical.

All these gardens are my feelings in your way sprinkle, sprinkle,
    My heart is lying in your way, O love just come gentle, gentle.

In this world, you are my love, shine, like stars twinkle, twinkle,
    All these gardens are my feelings in your way sprinkle, sprinkle.

Would you take me away from the boredom of this jungle, jungle?
    My heart is laying in your way, O love just come gentle, gentle.

No more pleased with a normal life, I want some miracle, miracle,
    All these gardens are my feelings in your way sprinkle, sprinkle.

You, everywhere in my dreams but now come physical, physical,
    My heart is laying in your way, O love just come gentle, gentle.

What a way you love, but now a change to be some lyrical, lyrical,
    All these gardens are my feelings in your way sprinkle, sprinkle.

How one can measure this love, it is beyond numerical, numerical,
    My heart is laying in your way, O, love just come gentle, gentle.

I am sorry for my deeds!

Keep up your love in my breath, as you are my need,
    Don't neglect to remove that oppression now to lead.

Strong winds against love but that love is my creed,
    Keep up your love in my breath, as you are my need.

Sorry for the years of agony, life is gone with a speed,
    Don't neglect to remove that oppression now to lead.

Why you are so pathetic, I had never any bad deeds,
    Keep up your love in my breath, as you are my need.

Are you a ghost! Or my host, then you let me read!
    Don't neglect to remove that oppression now to lead.

Please, don't hang off my love with ambitious greed,
    Keep up your love in my breath, as you are my need.

Why a jolly person was kept without his blessing seed,
    Don't neglect to remove that oppression now to lead.

Would you then help, the suppressed love to be freed?
    Keep up your love in my breath, as you are my need.

Deposed or Exposed?

Burning love in the heart but separation did expose it,
    The intent of worldly life has lost; someone deposed it.

Life was ideally perfect, to get ruined you supposed it,
    Burning love in the heart but separation did expose it.

Those words from lips were destructive as you cruise it,
    The intent of worldly life has lost; someone deposed it.

Couple was ideal but your better education did lose it,
    Burning love in the heart but separation did expose it.

I remember my efforts but you constantly opposed it,
    The intent of worldly life has lost; someone deposed it.

Tied hands with yours love, but contacts you closed it,
    Burning love in the heart but separation did expose it.

You pushed me practically to get insane, you assumed it,
    The intent of worldly life has lost; someone deposed it.

You announced last strike as you cunningly precede it,
    Burning love in the heart but separation did expose it.

I convinced by love, but you as a violence assumed it,
    The intent of worldly life has lost; someone deposed it.

Divine Help!

I screamed for help to the lord about financial stretch,
    Evil spells have turned my life like wet muddy pitch.

All mighty Lord blessed His mercy by the heavens sketch,
    Three exalted angels on the heavens presented holy touch.

How can I mistake divine signs with thanks much,
    Mighty Allah is the only one that help will ever teach.

After waking up its happening was realized in knowledge ditch,
    Only after three days its reality was proved at land Deutchs.

Oh Lord, accept my thanks for giving abundant financial switch,
    The glorious angels communicated in few words with less speech.

Allah, Thy humble servant; give me blessings for my humble reach,
    Bless us as wide, like high heavens and wide oceans loving beech.

Oh beloved lord, Thy blessing can't be compared with any match,
    We seek the help against misguidance, faith loss and wrath caught.

Everlasting.

True love in heart will never go away,
That beauty of the soul will never fade away.
    Love is hidden that hidden to convey,
    True love in heart will never go away.

Love remains young yet body turns to gray,
That beauty of the soul will never fade away.
    Chastity of love in terms to obey,
    True love in heart will never go away.

Love is not mathematical painful is its way,
That beauty of the soul will never fade away.
    Dreams, dreams now tell whatever to say,
    True love in heart will never go away.

Cold yesterday, waiting for the warmth of coming day,
That beauty of the soul will never fade away.
    Mortal life, each body is returning to the clay,
    True love in heart will never go away.

Three days of, life just one in hand to play,
Yes, that beauty of the soul will never fade away.

Plea for Mercy.

Oh Great Lord we seek refuge from Thy force,
Earth Quake, Tornado, Thunders Thy source.
    When the Angels swings their wings for a course,
    Tornado swallows its target on the ground of course.

Many shows, plus and minus charge in the clouds,
In their media they explain, to many crowds.
    Spiritual lack has embodied many doubts,
    Mercy on your nations they are dying like sprouts.

Have you heard the thundering sound, behind cloud!
On occasions Angels convey to the heavens very loud.
    I see, you don't see; I know you don't know,
    Find the truth, life is short; death brings final blow.

When the Jen raise to commit high treason,
The guardian Angels fire comet from the heaven.
    Many talks fallen rocks from galaxy in television,
    Misguidance, in such dark they brought ill invasion.

Further they well explain hot and cold air rotations,
Rainbow, storms and tornado further more expeditions.
    Jen and human once in trouble for divine mercy do the cry!
    Once in ease and power their little devil does they try.

Peace and salutations on heavens oh my Lord high,
We plea for Thy Mercy, you the only to be glorify.

Red Flower.

Remember the day when I planted red flower,
With blessings, fragrance will go much higher.
Merciful heaven will bring divine shower,
Touching emotions will bring real power.

Running feelings in the pulse to inspire,
Paradise is the only place for each desire.
Oh Lord, bless our efforts whatever we require,
Extinguish the greed which growing burning fire.

Peace and love to the world, all evil to retire,
Lost treasure of human as wisdom to acquire.
Oh Lord by mercy, give some knowledge of entire.
Thy mercy, Thy blessings is not a thing for a hire.

Well balanced Universe.

The clock is moving at the speed of the sun,
The mighty Lord established the universe to run.
    The moon, earth and planets with great strength done,
    With divine discipline the holy Angels work huge to thin.

Humans turned rebellious and raised their guns,
Greed became the motive, faith belief left to none.
    Many says monkey turned into human then,
    The very being forgotten only war of loss or win!

Do retreats from loss, divine mercy give everlasting fun,
New tech turned away the children from Lord the one.
    Exam is the world; you chose paradise or flame,
    Do not harm the fellows though yourself to blame.

Fallen from the heaven to the earth we do claim,
Oh Lord guide us to the truth we fallen in a shame.